BEYOND THE KNOWN

BY ROY MASTERS

Edited by Dorothy Baker

BEYOND THE KNOWN

Published by The Foundation of Human Understanding
Printed in the United States of America

For information, please direct your inquiry to:

The Foundation of Human Understanding
P.O. Box 34036, 8780 Venice Boulevard
Los Angeles, California 90034

or

P.O. Box 811, 111 N.E. Evelyn Street
Grants Pass, Oregon 97526

Cover design: Yuri Teshler
Cover illustration: Igor Bezenyan
Typography: Jeannette Papp

Library of Congress Catalog Card Number 88-83553
ISBN 0-933900-03-1

Contents

Prologue

"A man should learn to detect and watch that gleam of light which flashes across his mind from within, more than the lustre of the firmament of bards and sages. Yet he dismisses without notice his thought, because it is his.

"In every work of genius we recognize our own rejected thoughts; they come back to us with a certain alienated majesty. Great works of art have no more affecting lesson for us than this. They teach us to abide by our spontaneous impression with good-humored inflexibility most when the whole cry of voices is on the other side. Else, tomorrow a stranger will say with masterly good sense precisely what we have thought and felt all the time, and we shall be forced to take with shame our own opinion from another.

"We but half express ourselves, and are ashamed of that divine idea which each of us represents...God will not have his work made manifest by cowards."

Ralph Waldo Emerson
from "Self-Reliance"

1 The Identity Principle

Everyone in the world is suffering from an identity crisis. Something of ourselves is always leaving us and going into others and something of them is always coming into us. And strange as it may seem, this exchange process has something to do with our despair and our dying.

In our present state of mind, everyone is becoming us and we are becoming everyone else. The very coming together of two people sets in motion a strange process. Immediately one begins to lead; in the course of time, that leadership expresses itself in an increasing irritability that leads to tyranny and finally, to cruel domination.

Soon the tyrant personality begins to suffer feelings of guilt and anxiety for the demon role he feels obliged to play, while his hapless slave feels guilty for his weakness and his growing inferiority. Then, by adding resentment to his fear, the coward is compelled to go on giving power to the bully, thus enabling him to go on being more of a beast.

Sensing deep down that the way in which the victim is responding to him is largely responsible for the agonizing pain of his own power trip, the bully soon develops contempt for the sniveling coward. The underdog, not seeing his part in the creation of the evil that is lording it over him, simply dodges all responsibility for the situation and clings instead to the booby prize of judgment. So they continue to respond to each other in a deepening hypnotist-subject, vampire-zombie relationship.

In this Hell-on-earth feudal system we have brought upon ourselves through our compulsive emotional responses, we are driven to hurt, torture, and even kill one another. If they survive their exploitation, the demoralized downtrodden will often revolt and murder their masters. Surely we are all familiar with the "upmanship" tug-of-war being waged in our personal relationships. Multiply this by masses and governments, and you can see the underlying nature, the *modus operandi* of war and human suffering as it has existed from the beginning.

But let us leave aside the planetary effects of mass suffering and war for the moment, and turn our attention to the personal agony in the lives of the billions of people who make up the critical mass of fodder for the next holocaust, the one that is sure to come if we fail to learn our lesson and change the direction we have taken in our moral development. Think of the marriage relationships, business partnerships, heartless industrial feudal systems, the sly betrayals at the hands of neighbors, friends, brothers, and sisters. Let us look at the billions of willing slaves who are hopelessly caught up in weird religious cults. Wherever we look, we will see the same basic pattern at work.

This book is about the stress that kills, not the ordinary healthful stress that we face in sports, play, and physical labor, but a very special and deadly strain of stress that develops mysteriously into a living Hell, just from our coming together with one another in daily life.

In the typical husband/wife relationship, one partner always emerges as the dominant personality, and it is usually the woman who does so right from the start. Later, by imposing her authority on the offspring and impressing them with her power, she makes the children feel their inferiority. In doing so, she provides the basis for all the emotional traumas of rebellion and conformity in the children; she sets the stage for their future personal relationships. So time goes on, and soon, out into the world goes another generation of beings who are weak before the strong and strong before the weak. Among them, the men especially will be subject to "friendly," seductive women. Round and round it goes, from generation to generation, forming the feudal system of Hell on earth, multiplying suffering over the face of the world.

Wars will never end, sickness and disease will never come under our control, until we understand the mysterious flaw that exists in all our interpersonal relationships.

Somehow we are never able to relate to the real person; but we always seem ready to do business with the error that lurks inside him. Thus, we have problems, both with love and with hate.

For instance: If I lack the strength and wisdom to deal firmly with any trespass or indiscretion you might impose on me, no matter how petty it might be, then I *automatically and unconsciously encourage* the secret fault in you that gave rise to your wrong action. Now, you develop confidence in the flawed self that got away with the violation, and you are encouraged to take more liberties, both with me and with others. Unchallenged, you soon grow to be vain, pushy, violent, and vile; I, on the other hand, appear to be sweet, humble, and innocent by comparison with you. But I am not innocent. I am, in reality, part of your growing frustration and violence, even as you are part of the problem in me. My cowardice, as manifested in my failure to correct you on the spot, is responsible for the terrible effect my apparent martyrdom exerts over you.

The shock of your pressure-filled presence soon begins to get inside me through the cowardly resentment I harbor toward you. Your image begins to cross the border of my mind and soul, even to affect my innermost identity—the way I feel, serve, and grow. I feel conflict with my Real Self, and I feel guilty. I feel despair because, through guilt, I find myself compelled to serve the interests of other people rather than my own. I am confused because I am becoming externalized and emotionally suggestible. I am depressed because I am not living my own life. Instead, I am compelled to submit to your growing pressure, a pressure that I need in order to bolster my booby prize of blame and to feed the false righteousness that thrives on my secret judgment of your wickedness.

As time goes on, with both of us putting a finer edge on the role we have chosen to play rather than coming to grips with reality, we begin to drink, smoke, and drug ourselves senseless in order to ease the agony of living with the monsters we have helped each other to become. You have emotionally drained me, so that I'm beginning to be susceptible to disease. I have too little energy, and you have too much. Your pressures are becoming so unbearable that I want to put an end either to you or to myself.

We have given our money to the psychiatrists, and they have made everything worse. We resent all the friendly doctors for taking our money and not helping, for being just one more wrong relationship based on a misguided faith and adding fuel to our inner turmoil. We resent the tyranny of medicine and fall prey to more stress, frustration, violence—more of the guilt that drives us to need the help of a legion of Hell-based experts who become the next objects of our hatred. Our hearts are bursting in an environment of intrigue and betrayal. Pressures build up and knock out target organs. Our pancreas and thyroid can't handle the load; the liver and kidneys can't handle it either. Now, we have our own infirmities to resent. We are dying, fighting a losing battle with the enemy within. No one is himself anymore. We are one another. I am you, and you are I. And somewhere in the midst of all the confusion, voices are whispering, "Kill yourself; end it all. You deserve better than this. Rest."

Horrible? Yes. Irrevocable? No. We could reclaim our home in Paradise if only we could stop calling up the ectoplasm of Hell in our fellows, if only we could stop the Hell in ourselves from seeking out the love of the matching Hell in others.

The encounter begins innocently enough, with an affair or with friendship; but it always ends in fiendship. We are enamored with the instant recognition each of us bestows on the other. We offer ourselves as a living sacrifice to the power of "love" and a new lease on life, a new identity via the intimate relationship, and before we know it, the familiar pattern emerges. Remember the First Commandment? "Thou shalt have no other gods before me." Is God trying to teach us something about our relationships that we don't want to learn?

When we are not right within ourselves, we unconsciously elect outside "lesser" gods to accept us in a better light than we deserve, and they are the devils who lord it over us in the end. There is Hell to pay for the reassurance we need. Such friends are always enemies in disguise. Their nature gets inside us and begins to torment us from the new location. We begin to lose our own identity to them. They become us; we become them. It might not be so bad if their identity were a good identity, an improvement over the one we are trying to shed, but it never is.

You find yourself acting like the mother you loved and hated, turning around and doing to your own children what was done to you as a child, taking out your frustrations on the weak little ones, who also take on the old pattern by submitting to you and playing your old sacrificial-lamb role for "God's" approval. You are almost always attracted to the man or woman who most nearly duplicates the qualities of the mother or father who ruined you.

You cannot get away from the enemy because when someone else is not the enemy, the enemy is you. You are forever jumping from the frying pan into the fire, because any friend or authority who sympathizes with your troubles, anyone who distracts and consoles you, turns out to be the next enemy. Bad experience adds to bad experience, and personality adds to personality

6

inside you. Trauma builds on trauma, guilt on guilt, fear on fear, and when you see the hopelessness of it all, you fall prey to morbid depression.

As personal tyranny spreads and expresses itself in political and church dictatorships, rebel organizations form, complete with their own fiendship/friendship teachers and leaders.

The heartless cruelty of Russian Christian orthodoxy created the mad Frankenstein monster of communism. The slave practices of the selfish business world created the equally criminal unions with their "friendly" underworld heads of state.

What I am saying is that prideful people without Grace unconsciously draw Hell-based personalities into existence to attend and worship the needs of their falling egos. The immediate effect of their election is to encourage the wrong in us to feel right about itself. So we the people become more self-righteous, unaware, and insensitive to the harm we are doing to others as well as to the harm being done to ourselves by our friends, leaders, and lovers.

Our ego need drives us to go on giving power to a whole legion of problem solvers to lie-love us and so "save" us from the horrors of self-realization.

All those behavioral scientists, political and religious leaders who rise to the occasion of our needs become the next reason for our concern. Our problems are complicated by blind leaders who give us false answers, who live for no reason other than to perpetuate our need for their own vile existence. Once the alien agencies in human form establish themselves on earth, the entire purpose of their existence is to project a miserable Hell on earth from the Hell source they embody.

William Penn once said that if men did not find God, they would always be ruled by tyrants. Nations, like the men of which they are composed, cannot help but make the same mistake in electing their leaders.

What man ever marries a good woman? Surely, he only marries the one who makes him *feel* good. We select friends on the same basis. Soon they take liberties, and it is only a matter of time before they make our lives utterly miserable. It's no wonder that we have all become afraid of one another. We tear down our leaders and elect others. We divorce and marry, again and again. We drop old friends for new ones, to no avail. Whatever we do, it always ends the same way.

All around us, enemies are enemies and friends are enemies. Where can we turn? Is there no place to rest our weary heads? Must we always live in a snake pit? Where have the good people gone? Well, take heart. They are there, locked inside your fiend/friends and enemies, but they can't get out to communicate with you. You see, they feel the same way, but they can't reach you, any more than you can reach them.

When the pain of suffering pricks our ego to wake up, what is the first thing we do? Why, we go back to sleep to escape from realizing the truth. Unable to cope with the actual problem, we deal instead with our unwanted awareness of ever-present Truth. Simply by getting lost in our minds, in past and future concerns, we remain subject to the system, allowing many troubles and traumas to slip unnoticed through our sliding state of consciousness. We rarely see through to the cause of things because we are afraid to wake up and face Reality. Instead, we continue to deal stubbornly with effects by calling on the hypnotic presence of new personalities. The wrong in us uses the exciting presence of yet another overbearing person to help us forget our own weakness. We reminisce in the past, and we live in the future, thereby escaping from the Truth that shines in the present moment.

We deal with our problems by fighting old thoughts with new thoughts, covering negative thoughts with positive thoughts, but nothing works. Nothing works because we make sure to leave the door of our mind ajar, lest we miss out on some new tidbit of ego food. Our hungry, uncorrected, unloved self remains weak before the strong and strong before the weak; we hang onto the memories and personalities inside us that don't belong there. God! How they torment us with our need for their presence. Our need for their love is also our loathing for what they have done to us.

Now we try to fight off those leering images in our memory as our former "love" turns to hate. We get mad at those who have taken us over, and at ourselves for allowing it. We may even try to kill ourselves in an effort to purge our systems of the intruders. But no matter how hard we try, they are still there, stronger than ever, mocking our puny efforts. And when we try to repress from view the images of the enemy within, we lose sight of the enemy without. But he is still there, within and without, ever drawn to the parent spirit of fiendship and friendship. We continue to dramatize the will that is not our own through the self that is not our self. So here we are, lost, betrayed, miserable, guilty, compulsive, confused, and at a loss to know why.

The monster of the id, the false identity deep in our minds, soon becomes the pressure source and starts to boss us around with a will that we cannot resist even though we know that it is not our own. Just as other people stress us, the "other mind" stresses us, driving us to desperation and draining our vitality. And we always make the same mistake by running away from the painful, but redeeming, presence of our conscience into the place in our mind where past and future exist, into the embrace of Hell.

So, you see, the basic problem of mankind is one of identity, inasmuch as man was created originally to express the will and purpose of the creative over-shadowing Spirit. When he took it upon himself to be his own god, he broke the bond with his Creator and took on an attitude of ego that will never admit it is wrong.

When we cease to be influenced by good, then we fall by default under the influence of evil. And evil, operating through the human agencies we become, impresses us through dominating personalities. We take upon ourselves *their* spirit, *their* will, *their* natures. Women tend to become masculine, and men tend to become feminine.

Now, since we seem to have lost our identity somewhere in the world, we tend to look to the world to give it back to us, and that is when we make the fatal mistake of putting beautiful people on a pedestal and bowing down and worshipping them. Unconsciously, of course, we hope to take on their good image and apparent virtues in exchange for our own bad ones. It doesn't work, of course, but once you become involved with a personality, such as a religious or cult leader, you find it difficult to see what is really going on. You begin to resemble your guru, not only in outward appearance of hypocrisy and phoniness, but also in spirit.

Strangely enough, true salvation also involves an exchange process, a shedding of the worldly personality to take on, and reflect, the personality of God. But that is a far cry from claiming the godhead for ourselves, a delusion we often implement by setting up some other god to worship, thereby knowing ourselves as god-*makers*, gods *over* gods.

For true salvation, we must seek out and find the Divine personality through Whom we can be reconciled, and through Whom our natures can be altered.

Salvation exists in the Eternal Now within us. This book is dedicated to bringing you back to the present moment, to the Now, where the Truth lives always, where we can experience His presence, where He can take our sins upon Himself and give us back our bright nature to bond with His purity.

The wicked powers that be are desperate to keep you from the knowledge of the way. The power of Evil on earth comes from people-idolatry and image worship; in other words, from the vile practice of giving people good images of themselves.

The Devil knows all about the weaknesses and needs of our proud egos. His agents strut around like actors on the stage, playing the god role you cast them in for the purpose of enjoying your own godship over them. But all the while, you are becoming evil, and evil is becoming you. You are becoming diseased and broken in spirit, and your sexually confused carcass has been taken over by the very spirit of Evil itself. To say it more simply, your problem is that you are lost between your ears, where you are completely subject to forces in your environment.

The solution is to come back to the objective state. Find your way back to the Now, where Reality waits patiently to change your nature and your ways. God does not give up His secrets through the workings of our minds. He reveals them through the still soul who stands humbly in the Now present.

Through effort, we involve ourselves with the workings of our imagination, and we call that process "creative." But out of those imaginings come the devilish ideas that deceive us with a sick sense of power. And all the while we are absent-minded; that is, absent from the presence of the Mind that created us, we allow alien identities to slip in unnoticed and stand unholy in the place of the Holy.

Man is half, woman is half. Correctly related, they could make a whole person. But through the process of using and corrupting each other, something of the male goes to the female, and something of the female goes to the male. So, fallen males are excited by the prospect of getting back the missing part of themselves and becoming men again, but that is where they make their big mistake and lose even more of themselves. That is the trap.

The missing ingredient, the only one that counts, is the bond with the Creator. If we were not so busy, trying egotistically to get back our lost wholeness from the world, and making up from others what we have lost through sin, we might repent of our original sin and be saved.

2 The Captive Mind

Your mind is stressing you to death. All the memories that come back to taunt you cause your body to react as though the past were repeating itself over and over again.

Foolish people try to reverse the negative effect that their memories have on their bodies by reminiscing in a nostalgic way; that is, they recall only good experiences in order to hang onto good feelings in the present, but alas, they are obliged to spend more and more time amid the fantasies of their minds, prettying up the past to drag it into the "future" of the present. They are degenerating in the process.

We cope with the fear of the future by running toward memories of the past. With nothing to look forward to, we go back in time to the childishness that characterizes senility. As you succumb to this vile practice, your memories excite you and drag you down, draining away your energy. Down, down your ego goes, back to the beginning, to the time when things were better and you were more innocent.

But to know the true innocence of a new life's beginning, you must go forward to meet your true self, and forward is not necessarily somewhere ahead of you. It lies just beyond time itself, in the moment when the Light shines within you.

Past and future are devices the ego uses to escape from reality, and they exist only in the mind. Your problem is that you live so much in the past and the future that you fail to meet the present moment correctly.

Your thought world is filled with past and future, but the only time you have in which to see clearly the truth of anything is the present, the time that *is*, now. The reason you are making such a mess of your life is that you don't know how to live calmly and objectively in that present.

You cannot govern your own life properly as long as you allow yourself to be subtly guided by the phantoms of your imagination. As long as your consciousness, your ego self, remains lost in thought, imprisoned in a dungeon of dreams, no meaningful change can take place in your life.

Strong emotions stir up vivid thoughts that can hold your attention so captive that you fail to see where you are going, and when you can't see where you are going, you have accidents. Being constantly upset and preoccupied affects the way in which you see people and opportunities, so you make bad judgments, and the bad judgments lead to more frustration, more debilitating reactions to stress. Your emotional upsets drain you of energy and you become run-down. Your health suffers, and disease claims you.

While it is true that emotions can distort your thinking, your mixed-up thinking is equally capable of creating an unhealthy emotional state. (Which came first, the chicken or the ego?) The truth of the matter is that as long as your consciousness is totally involved with its thinking, you remain caught in a vicious cycle that can't be broken, one that will break you, mentally, emotionally, and physically.

Once you are able to free yourself from the destructive influence of the dream reality, you will inherit the true reality in a fully aware state, and it will come to bear on your unconscious thinking with a powerful force. Immediately, you stop being a victim of your imagination. You stop being so afraid, guilty, and upset.

The simple act of becoming objective to the whirlpool of your thoughts exerts a fantastic power over your emotions and supplies you with an unending source of direction. It also leads you to the virtues of patience and love that will keep you calm through life's cruel trials and subtle temptations.

Ancient wise men, the patriarchs, the great Hebrew and Christian mystics, lived in what they called the Light. They always knew intuitively what to do and what to say; they faced no problems they couldn't solve, because they were not lost in the dark realm of imagination as people are today. They knew the great secret of life, a secret that the false religious teachers and ambitious political leaders have hidden from the people in order to exploit and control them while keeping themselves safe from detection.

Now, your modern gurus, the so-called problem solvers, give you the kinds of answers that only breed new problems along with a debilitating dependency on themselves to "solve" them. The confusion and decadence you see all around you, the futility and meaninglessness of your own life are all the result of your not knowing how to see clearly and independently as humans should; instead, you see and react as animals.

Your feelings make you think, and your thinking makes you feel; around and around you go in a squirrel cage of passion, rage, and confusion. The culture of which you are so proud has deliberately "educated" you to look to your feelings and imagination for answers, the very places where answers can never be found and where you can only lose your real Self. You have been had.

It's time for you to wake up out of your deep sleep, from dreams that lead to all those nightmare realities you are afraid to face and that drag you back to more dreaming, worrying, and escaping from reality.

My purpose in writing this book is to introduce you to an ancient Judeo-Christian meditation technique that will help you, the sincere seeker, to separate your conscious mind from the confusion of your thoughts. When you learn to observe yourself calmly without resenting anything you see there, without struggling against memories of failure and weakness, you will see something marvelous happen. Your problems will come to resolution *of themselves,* without your having to make any effort to resolve them.

The technique I teach is not a form of mind control, nor is it aimed at emotional suppression; its only purpose is to bring you to a state of awareness and objectivity. Up to this point, your ambitions have led you into the habit of dreaming about what you want, and that fixation with dream stuff has blocked your awareness of what you were getting into. You have fallen into the machinery of your own mind. Down there, you are fixated to self-destructive and self-defeating thoughts of relief. Your mind is running away with itself, dangerously trying to find answers that can reveal themselves to you only when you are fully awake.

You must realize that the mental/emotional and emotional/mental state you have fallen into is the direct result of your being lost in your thoughts. Only one remedy is open to you, and that is to become *objective,* so that you can see beyond the mental/emotional mist. Only then will you be able to see clearly the part you have been playing in the creation of your problems.

Be aware that you do not gain mastery over your emotions by struggling with them, or with the thoughts you have been using to rationalize them. All you have to do is wake up and separate your conscious mind from the stream of unconscious thinking you have fallen into. I am stretching out my hand to help you up to another level of awareness, above the ordinary conscious state, so that you may gain control over the way you feel and think.

All your bad reactions to life's experiences are the result of your not being properly aware, being too preoccupied with your own mind and body, with study, goals, and the advice of problem solvers. You are never more powerless than you are when you are immersed in a whirlpool of thought, especially when things go wrong, for then you step up your mental activity and get sucked in. In your present condition, you cannot possibly realize how much power you would gain from being objectively aware.

Rarely, if ever, would you err in your judgments or

your relationships with people if you were objective to your thinking. Your enlightened consciousness would develop perfect dominion over the course your life must take; unruly passions would be a thing of the past. The moment something becomes too important to you or you allow yourself to get upset, you begin to lose awareness. When you are too ambitious, you tend to lose sight of real values; you forget what is wise as you become involved with thinking about what you want out of life.

Too much ambition always plunges your conscious self into a dreamlike state where you are unable to see to the right or to the left, and you begin to make errors of judgment. The blind ego, fueled by the pride that made it ambitious in the first place, refuses to realize the error of its ways. How can a proud ego admit to error? So you solve that problem by turning your back on reality, by willfully losing all awareness of what went wrong. You do that by giving all your attention to worry, fantasy, or dreams of a new goal.

Becoming lost in the machinery of your thinking makes you vulnerable to emotional stress from two directions. One, you start reacting with frustration, resentment, and fear to the mistakes you find yourself making from day to day; and two, you find yourself overreacting to memories of past mistakes that keep coming back to haunt you. Stress is debilitating, whether it attacks from the outside or the inside, from the present environment or the memory of past failure.

Images that come to mind through daydreams or as the result of reacting badly to stress (temptation, really) can affect you every bit as much as the physical environment does. They can threaten, deceive, anger, excite. They can even drain you of energy, leaving you run-down and subject to disease. Surely you have experienced the reliving of a past trauma in your mind, and reacting to it as though it were actually happening to you, over and over again. Your thoughts actually triggered emotional reactions. No doubt you even resented the troublesome thoughts, and that made everything worse. Then, you probably tried to stay busy to avoid thinking about your problem. You might even have suppressed the memories altogether, but the process continued on a lower level of consciousness. Sooner or later, you had so much to suppress that your thoughts and feelings bubbled up from below and overwhelmed you. Bad feelings, carrying with them bad thoughts, are always stronger than your attempts at positive thinking; and there you go again, lost in thought, frightened, depressed, helpless, and hopeless.

In varying degrees, we are all lost in an Alice Through the Looking Glass, upside-down world of imagination; we just don't know how to get out over the wall of thought. During the time when your delusions and imagined needs affected you as though they were of the real world, you believed and followed what appeared to be meaningful knowledge in order to make important decisions; but somewhere down the line, you came face-to-face with disillusionment.

How many times have you wakened in a cold sweat to escape from a dream phantom or from sinking in a swamp? There is no way you could have tempered your fearful reactions, for when you are not fully aware, fully conscious, the dreamworld is your only reality, and it compels your lost ego-self to react to it.

You wander around in varying states of conscious-ness, mostly, alas, in a dream state. First you plan the action in which you hope to find fulfillment; then, you start planning your escape from the mistake of plan-ning. As long as you live in the dream state, the only information available to you is dream stuff and it always misleads you. As a result, you fall prey to bad reactions. You get caught in a vicious cycle: Your emotional reactions spin your thoughts, and your thoughts pull you in to live among the images of your mind. Soon, the images themselves upset you. Here is where you make the big mistake. Instead of waking up to solve your problem in a fully aware state, you strug-gle against the dream feelings with dream answers. You try to change your thinking; or, because you are so externalized, you try to change the circumstances that affect your emotions and your thinking. You worry, and you try to rearrange your thoughts to make yourself look right. It's enough to drive you mad.

Imagination grows as you feed it with bad reactions to stress, until the potpourri of stress-based impressions that get inside you grow to unwieldy proportions. Allow me to illustrate the way your imagination can destroy you if you are not its master as the result of being awake. Take a typical dream scene: You are sur-rounded by demon doctors who want to cut you up into little pieces. Armed with poison-filled syringes, they are chasing you around the hospital, but you can-not escape because you can't find your shoes. If it doesn't occur to you to wake up, it is probably because you fail to realize that you are dreaming. The more

20

vivid your imagination is, the more you, the observer, are involved in it, the more power it has to keep your normal consciousness submerged to such a deep level that you are totally cut off from reality. In such a case, the dream appears to be the reality.

You tend to look on your fantasies as innocent little excursions to a fairy-tale world where you are "master of all you survey," a refuge from the dog-eat-dog world that so obstinately fails to recognize your true worth. So you fail to see the danger inherent in these excursions from reality. Eventually, your emotion-based fancies will completely distort the way you see life. You will not only react foolishly to what your tricky imagination tells you is real, but you will read meaning into things in such a way that you cause bad reactions in the people around you. As a result, the people become a problem, a stress that you never had before. Haven't you ever misjudged someone and then felt so guilty that you just had to go on believing they were wrong in order to escape from the truth that you had indeed misjudged them?

Your world of imagination is "alive" with an assortment of *unquestioned beliefs*, cultural conditioning factors, and conflicting ideas that have arisen from frustration, futility, failure, rage, and fear. Being prey to your thoughts (thoughts being your reality) compels you to respond violently to any kind of information as though it were true. But if dreams and imaginings are your only reality, how can you question anything? How can you find any meaningful answers? You cannot. Henceforth, you must pluck your answers from the dream fabric of your escape world. All your problems come from this habit of drawing on memories and delusions of the mind. You do strange, contradictory things, but since you cannot see those contradictions, you confuse and hurt those you are supposed to love. As a result, you get angry, then guilty, until your guilt causes you to withdraw from the reality of your actions into the "reality" of daydreams.

A spiritual reality lurks behind every dream, a reality that spells tragedy to your soul, a reality that you are afraid to face. Dream long enough, my friend, and you will find yourself jumping from the frying pan into the fire. You will seek your usual escape from tragedy and failure in the world of dreams, only to meet the awful reality behind the dream.

Of course, all you have to do to get away from dream monsters and tragedies that have their origin in imagination is wake up. But how many of us do? We are like the dreamer running from the evil doctors, still looking for our shoes. Either we *will not* wake up, or we don't know how.

The human journey through life nearly always begins with an egocentric dream and ends in tragedy and spiritual nightmares. Dwelling too much in the world of imagination can be a terminal disease in itself. The more problems you create by not being aware, the more afraid your ego is to face up to the actual results of your failure to stay awake, and the more you tend to descend into the world of imagination for escape "answers" from the phantom saviors you have conjured up out of your ego's need to be saved from guilt and to be cloaked with innocence. Dreaming is the actual villain that leads to the real tragedy, the real failure that we are afraid to face. The end of the line is the spirit of horror lurking behind the nightmare dream. There is a flip side to thought, another side to the ectoplasm of thinking, and that is where its architect, the evil reality, lurks.

You cannot govern your emotions or take control of your life as long as you remain a prisoner in a thought world. You must begin to thread your way out of the world of imagination and come up to the Light; you must stir from your trance-like state, for only above your thoughts can you find new and meaningful alternatives to the way you are going, alternatives that will save you from the horror of sinning and dying. Remember, there is nothing wrong with you that waking up, becoming fully conscious, can't cure.

How can you function intelligently if you are perpetually lost in a sea of thought? You can't. You must find a completely objective presence of mind in order to break down the power of deception. If you can't wake up, it's because you won't, or you don't know how. And if you don't know how, let me teach you, through the meditation tapes that are available from The Foundation of Human Understanding. They will teach you how to separate your conscious Self from the thinking, feeling mind, so that you may come to know the Truth that can set you free.

Thoughts can be dealt with, but not dreams. In dreams, you are not the master, but the victim. The thoughts that rise up in your fantasies from below, seeming to have no purpose but to serve you, are really your Lord. But how can you know that, as long as you are so busy escaping from the Truth? Why else are you dreaming? Evil spirits, masters of deception, disguised in loving and religious images, are your comforters and "saviors," and as long as you are vain (openly or covertly), they will be your reality. It is your love of deception that draws dream phantoms to embrace you and draw you reciprocally to themselves. Finally, when the veil parts, you will see the evil spirit behind them.

No one ever cared enough to show you the way. The vested interests of society have never wanted to help you. They have only wanted to put you to sleep and exploit you in your ignorance. Horrible as these tangible external realities are, they are often cloaked in respectability. They are the "friends," who teach you to be ambitious. They lead you in your trance state to their master and maker, the Devil himself.

The moment you are willing to become aware of the fact that you are dreaming, in that moment, you will no longer be floating in the dream. As you continue to observe the dream as a dream, you see a transformation take place: it becomes thought, no longer real. Seeing the dream as a delusion of thought, and observing the deceiver behind the deception, you are no longer confused. You do not follow. You are no longer compelled to react and obey. You begin to take charge of your own life. You begin to function from a wordless, common-sense knowing, and a new world begins to work itself through you. At last, life is meaningful.

Just be careful not to develop a false sense of confidence from the fact that you are making some changes in your belief system—like dropping one friend for another, or switching investments. The impetus behind these changes might be coming from your same old dreamworld; you must not regard them as a sign that you are waking up. But as soon as you separate from your imagination to see the dream as thought, the true open-eyed awareness will save you from continuing in the direction the dream "reality" was taking you. You will no longer react with terror and hopelessness to the shadowy things of your imagination that you were not even able to share with anyone else, not even for the sake of seeing them "exorcised."

Just become perfectly conscious of what you are doing, and you will immediately begin to know for certain what is wise or unwise, real or unreal, deceptive and emotional or logical and objective. When you develop the confidence that comes from not being a victim of deception, you will automatically respond in a right way. You will no longer experience traumatic shocks. You *will* know the marvelous power that comes with being awake, the power to respond in a right way as the result of being able to *see* what the right way *is*.

People lose their power to take advantage of you when they see you watching them calmly from beyond your thoughts. They will know that their game is up and you are their master when you fail to respond to their schemes.

Once you are committed, you will find it impossible to continue in the error of your ways and hang onto your consciousness at the same time. Slowly, your guilts, dark moods, fits of rage and anxiety, will diminish. You will be less able to hurt, or to be hurt by, others, and death will lose its sting. Even your nervous habits will give you up. You simply won't be tempted by the vices you once found so appealing, like drinking, smoking, taking drugs, or whatever else you once turned to for relief.

A fantastic power dwells in the objective state of consciousness to affect you and everything around you for the good. Until you learn to "be still and know" that power, you are doomed to be led by your imagination and the demons beyond it.

Emotion-based mental activity is strangely compelling because we are so guilty, and the only relief from guilt, other than repentance, lies in escape from the awareness of it. We manage to do that (or so we think) by delving deeper into our mind stuff with a greater determination to plan and scheme and make things work out, to "get even." After all, "thinking will make it so," or so we think. The nagging, barely conscious awareness that it *won't* drives us to worry, and all worry can do is set off another flurry of mental activity.

In the beginning, your hope, a primitive kind of faith, was that your dreams would lead you to the reality of a material, ego-satisfying paradise of success and happiness, but they never do. As failure follows failure, you become upset and frustrated, and your frustration drives you to a constant preoccupation with the defense mechanisms of thinking, dreaming, and worrying. You may even see more tragedy ahead, the inevitable end of the road you have chosen to take, but you don't know how to turn around. When you try, it's like driving with the brakes on. You keep "willing" all of your schemes to "work," but you will be caught in a vicious cycle until you become committed to waking up.

Your ego's need to escape from reality, the truth about its condition, is what gives the world of thought its magnetic power to suck you in. Thought whirlpools are terribly inviting, fascinating, and soothing to the ego. For a little while, they can make you feel innocent and secure. But only for a little while, for every dream carries the seed of future shock and is a bad trip that will bottom out on the hard rock of reality. All your bad reactions to life are having a bad effect on your physical nature and on your very identity.

The ego that dreams and schemes and sets things in motion sets all the wrong things in motion. If you were not so involved in your thinking, you could *know the truth* about things. You could see clearly because your perception would not be clouded by conditioning, training, and emotional prejudice. You would be free to do what is wise.

There are no problems in Reality for the person who faces it from an objective point of view. Reality poses a problem to you only because you are lost in your thoughts, busily shaping a counterfeit image of reality to bring it closer to your pride's desire. As long as you stay so busy with the do-it-yourself project of re-creating Reality, you are estranging yourself from the courage required to face it as it is. That courage would be available to you in the objective state of awareness that I hope to bring you to.

Worry is one of the favorite escape mechanisms for those who are not ready to face themselves. It is a pre-occupation with the guilts, anxieties, and resentments that well up from past memories, a kind of "cud chewing" that keeps one's attention riveted to the problems of the past as an escape from meeting the present. The proud ego looks on worry as a kind of loving concern, which it most certainly is not.

A truly loving concern springs from a bright, objective state of consciousness called presence of mind. It is never ambitious. The ambitious person worries, and sees only problems, whereas the loving person shows his concern by looking only to the solution. Actually, there are no big problems in life, only a lot of little ones that accumulate when a person loses awareness and starts responding like a lost soul, with resentment, toward other lost souls.

You probably fell into your thinking as the result of a preoccupation with some prideful goal. Then, as the gap widened between reality and the dream, you began to react against the truth of your having been deceived, and your frustration at being lost led to resentment and worry over the means of getting out of the trap you had fallen into. But to worry is to dream more deeply, to become subject to the demon of worry.

Instead of giving in to worry, which never helps, you must allow the reason for your predicament to catch up with you. If you fail in this, it is because your pride insists on struggling willfully, without understanding. The struggle will only involve you more deeply in the mire of your own thoughts and will lead to bigger problems.

It is hard, I know, to wake up from sinking in your thinking and drowning in your dreams. If you are prideful, you will need all your schemes and dreams to distract you from seeing the guilt that your ambition has created for you. You will crave stimulants, such as alcohol, drugs, music, and tobacco to keep you excited and upset, to spin your thoughts at a faster pace, to insure your remaining emotionally secure, safely locked up in your delusions, incapable of realizing how weak, lost, and helpless you really are. A prideful person never wants to be aware. He rejects the gift of presence of mind because awareness would show him what a fool he is. In his dreaming he never has to be wrong; he never needs to repent. Too proud to experience guilt graciously, he goes on scheming and dreaming, fancying himself to be a god or a martyr.

Proud people need illusion and deception to make them feel secure. You will be hated for any attempt to change them, for your awareness pierces their dream bubble and tends to wake them up. You cannot help them, but don't let them cause you to doubt yourself. Leave them alone to die in their folly. Leave them to the demon of their dreamworld.

If you have had the stomach to read this far, you can not be one of those dreamers. You are seeking your true identity, your lost state of dignity and awareness. You may even be tuning in to my radio programs and meditating by my technique. Or you may be one of the cautious souls who have to test the water, toe by toe, before jumping in. Whoever you are, and wherever you come from, I know that I can help you on the road to understanding. Welcome aboard.

3 The Hypnosis of Stress

What do most of us mean by "the struggle of life"? Isn't it the struggle we are obliged to wage against powerful people and destructive thoughts? No sooner have we finished one contest than we are left with another, the bad aftertaste of our own thoughts.

Your reaction to the stress people put on you throws you into a hypnotic state, and in that state, you are compelled to say and do things that you will regret later when you return to full awareness. At this point, of course, it is your own awareness that looks like the enemy because of the anxiety you feel when you realize what you have done. You can drive yourself to distraction with your efforts to "rewrite the script," or to sweep the whole incident under the carpet as though it had never taken place.

Every problem you have is linked directly to your being unable to cope with pressure; you simply cannot think or function properly when you are excited. You can prove that statement for yourself just by thinking back to a recent stressful situation that you handled poorly. It may have been with a boss you hate, or with someone who means too much to you. You will see that simply by recalling the scene to your mind, you will undergo the same sensations you felt at the time, hypnotically. Your heart races, and there you are, lost in a trance-like daydream, still trying to find the right words, or the courage you would need in order to say them.

You can not cope with life if you are constantly absorbed in your thoughts; and the people around you probably know that you need full awareness to deal with them effectively. Why else would they keep you upset all the time? The manipulators of the world grow strong on the weakness of the masses of people who can't cope and are thus reduced to staying lost in their mind, in fantasy, confusion, and escape, with the aid of such stimulants as drugs, alcohol, tobacco, and food.

If you were able to face the world calmly, without resentment, nothing could move you off center or threaten your self-respect. It is resentment that hands you over to the enemy and destroys your peace of mind. Do I hear you saying to yourself, "Yes, but..."? Pride specializes in "yes, but" excuses for the fallen ego, like "Yes, but he was ten times my weight; I *had* to run," or "Yes, but he made me so mad that I *had* to attack him." In your pride, the very Truth that can save you becomes the enemy you feel called upon to defeat. (Well, I have to save face, don't I? How often have you "justified" yourself with those words?)

Your wrong reactions to stress enslave you to the evil behind every stress that challenges you. The emotional state that you allow the environment to whip you into testifies to your failing as a person, because it carries you away from reason and drives you into the rationalizations of your mind for refuge. There, you are compelled to play the scene over and over again, "seeing" the "enemy" in ever more vicious ways in order to justify your unreasonable reaction, whether it had been to run or to fight. Like a lawyer, you keep strengthening the case against the adversary. If you can keep the focus of attention on him, you think you can avoid facing the truth of your own guilt. Be honest, now. How many little incidents have you managed to forget ever occurred, simply because you couldn't bear to relive the shoddy part you played in them? Your pride wouldn't allow it.

The problems we all share, the tragedies in our lives, begin when we realize that the way we handled a stress situation has left us confused and guilty. And we can't handle the guilt. So we remove the one factor that could save us in the next encounter, and the next, and that is the plain, open-eyed, clear *seeing* of our failure to behave according to principle. We were given our chance, and we turned our backs on it. But we're still not ready to give up our pride. We figure that by refusing to *see* the wrong, we can "not see" it out of existence entirely.

Once our failure to deal with stress has driven us to the world of thought for refuge, we come up with all kinds of wrong answers and face-saving compensations. We become vulnerable to suggestion, and once a suggestion has been planted in a person's mind, there is no way to stop it from hatching out. The struggle you put up against suggestion succeeds only in driving it deeper into the fabric of your psyche; it wears you out until you can fight no more. So you give in to the suggestion with a kind of cosmic feeling that no other course was available to you. It was your karma, your manifest destiny.

You give in so completely to the suggestions of your manipulators, albeit unconsciously, that you are forevermore compelled to live within the boundaries of the world they have laid out for you. They become the "culture" in which you form your ideas of the "rightness" of things in the laboratory of your unconscious mind. No woman will look like "right" marriage material, for instance, until you find one just like the mother who set you up to be manipulated when you were young. You marry your corrupter for the same reason that cannibals elect cannibal kings to guide them in their sleep and keep them asleep, lest they discover what they have allowed their culture to do to them.

"I am what I am," sang Popeye, the sailor man, and I can hear the echo everywhere. Can't you? Once a person has capitulated to the stress of his culture, he wears the identity it has given him like a badge of honor; he no longer has to look at that identity objectively, explain it, apologize for it, or repent of it.

People are loyal to the stress that overcomes and converts them. But if you look carefully, you will see treachery afoot in human loyalties. When we humans give in to another person's pressure, it is usually with the idea that we can somehow use that capitulation as a means of conquest, a way of lulling the lord and master into a false sense of security while we quietly take over his power. It is the favorite weapon of the weak and disenfranchised. A man in a man's world thinks he can win by intimidation, but a woman in a man's world knows that her best chance at winning lies in capitulation. She can cling to a man and suck the life out of him until, lo and behold, she becomes a man herself. Of course, this stratagem can backfire badly when the man refuses to be cajoled and reacts with violence; but even then, an abused woman will submit to an incredible amount of torture before screaming for help.

We often express our rebellion against one person by conforming to another, especially if the other is highly disapproved of by the one we are rebelling against. Your children, for instance, will gladly do for strangers what they won't do for you. Or they will do everything you told them not to do when they fall under the influence of some neighborhood good-for-nothing.

The stress of excitement you feel when somebody likes you counters the stress you feel when you are hated. Either way, you are compelled to react, either with conformity or with rebellion. What compels you to react is an evil that has invaded the person who is stressing you—even the well-meaning one, for we should not have to look to one another for love, and, of course, the one whose purpose is to upset you into doing something stupid. Either way, the evil gets to you through your reactions to it.

Once you begin to react, you are compelled to obey, and whether we realize it or not, this slavishness is something we are all struggling with in some way. It is responsible for much of our suffering, anxiety, and guilt.

Almost every one of us is functioning from a source of direction other than his own intuitive source of reason. And it's the failure to "take charge" of ourselves, only half realized, that accounts for our conflict, anxiety, and guilt feelings. We feel guilty because we *are* guilty, but a stubborn pride forbids us to trace the guilt to its source.

Everyone is wandering around in the grip of some sort of hypnosis that was brought on by reactions to stress. We speak and we act from what we have been programmed to say and to do. We cling fast to the beliefs that have been laid on us, refusing to entertain another person's opposite beliefs, not because we have a commonsense objection to them, but because pride compels us to stand up for ourselves just the way we are—meaning just the way our culture has re-created us through our identification with it.

If you allow yourself many little lapses in behavior, like white lies, outright distortions or face-saving omissions of fact, you are guilty of a secret dishonesty. And to the extent that you fail to act in accordance with what you know is right in your heart, you become defensive against Truth and vulnerable to stress. Your many little ego indulgences keep you and everybody around you in a state of confusion. You rise to the temptation in *every* stress because your dishonesty strips you of resistance to pressure. All you have left in you to resist *with* is the energy that springs from a reaction to the stress itself, rather than the energy that would well up inside you from an independent source of strength if you were loyal to the Truth. Each succeeding reaction to stress adds another touch to the alien "you" that stress is creating in its own image, a "you" that is easily controlled by outside pressures.

Outright stealing and cheating are not the only forms of dishonesty. When I speak of dishonesty, I speak of the little games you are playing with yourself, such as your refusal to admit your failure after you have been tempted or corrupted. Or the excuses you make to yourself for going after anything you want, tooth and claw, with complete disregard for the feelings and rights of others. Once you have given up principles in exchange for material gain, and have become hardened in your pride, you will want to fall asleep to what you have become. You won't want to see that your desires, and what you are doing to fulfill them, are both wrong—dead wrong.

Anyone can tell when he is awake that he is not fast asleep. However, there is a state of consciousness between the waking and the sleeping states, through which you pass on the way to either extreme. The person who gets stuck in that state is hypnotized. I am not yet clear as to why this hypnotic state exists and what positive value it may have; but I do see how your own mind can be used against your best interests and how you can be thoroughly exploited and demoralized through it. There must be a natural purpose for this state of mind, provided you don't get stuck at that level. I know that when you are free to move out of its sphere of influence at will, whatever natural purpose exists for it will operate in your favor.

The states of consciousness that concern us at this time are sleep, hypnosis, awakeness, and awareness. Your conscious self can live on any of these levels, but it can function perfectly only on the level where it belongs, and that is the aware, objective state. In any of the other states you will experience compulsion, guilt, and anxiety. Just being awake will never do; you must go beyond that. You must become aware. If you fail in this, you are in danger of being sucked into deeper hypnotic states and falling prey to their subtle suggestions both in waking and sleeping moments.

The first thing the meditation exercise will do for you is bring you up through the layers of hypnosis to the stage of being fully awake. But that stage does not, of itself, give you full control over your own life; what it does is help you understand the mistakes you have been making and enable you to realize the existence of an ultimate state of consciousness that you must reach in order to experience a problem-free existence.

Your descending consciousness has never known this perfected, objective state, because all you inherited as your birthright was the potential of an ordinary state of awakeness; your ego mind grew up locked into that level. It was there that you saw how vulnerable and mortal you were. Later, you were traumatized or pressured into losing that awakeness, and you began to withdraw into yourself. You began to shrivel away from reality and do battle with your problems in the dark, without the light to guide you to their solution.

As your consciousness fell to lower levels, you became increasingly self-conscious. Higher states of consciousness beckon your ego to rise out of the mire and become whole and complete; but you hang back because your ego feels strangely threatened by the truth, governed as it is by an inherited pride. It is pride that causes you to reject the reality that makes you feel self-conscious and renders you more and more vulnerable to stress, and that keeps you from seeing the truth of your condition.

If you are not lost in the process of losing awareness,

what you are faced with is the truth, the truth about yourself. Your ego discovers how little it is, by the light of the Truth that is so much more. You begin to see, also, that there is something not quite right about the way you exist physically. You are very mortal, indeed, and as long as you remain conscious, you know by the presence of Reality that you are; but because this knowledge is too painful for your pride to deal with, you take refuge in your mind. There, your ego draws a curtain against the light and you begin to think you are something that you are not.

In the hypnotic state, the mind computes the information it receives into a compulsion to act. Animals enjoy a similar kind of automatic response, and in their case, it is completely in accordance with natural law. When it comes to humans, however, this type of response signals a descent from the natural level of consciousness on which we were intended to live. In other words, it is actually possible for the conscious spiritual self to live on any of the levels of the mind, including the hypnotic one that a person tends to pass through on the way to the sleeping and waking states, but that does not mean that a person should voluntarily forsake the objective aware state through which he expresses his allegiance to his Creator. Indeed, the perfectly aware man or woman never falls into a deep sleep, but hangs on to a "sentry" level of awareness to stand guard over him while he rests his body.

In the absence of true knowledge, your conscious ego self tends to be caught up with, even drawn to, whatever it is that the body is experiencing. If you can sleep, you get lost in sleep, and when you are awake, you are not fully aware. Awake, you are still under the influence of unconscious thoughts that are coming to the surface as the result of partially digested learning experiences.

On a more positive note, I strongly suspect that the hypnotic state of mind is where understanding translates into positive behavior. However, as long as your conscious ego self is locked into that state, the only suggestions you can actually receive must come through the senses. When you do get your bearings and begin to take direction from a true understanding, you are no longer operating out of compulsion. What can be more natural than doing what you see to be wise?

Just remember that if you can be induced into a hypnotic state, you will be operating under some outside control. You will not be your own person. You may not see that you have been enslaved by another will, simply because you don't want to see it. And as long as you don't see what has happened to you, you don't question your compulsions or see anything wrong with the way you are acting. But if I can snap you out of the hypnotic state and bring you back to a full awareness, you will begin to be informed by a higher understanding, whose positive suggestion will lead you to positive action.

You experience the pain of the compulsive way only when you are locked into it, and even then, you may not see what is wrong. Most people who are hypnotized fail to see their behavior as the acting out of a compulsion, because they can see only what they have been programmed to "see." Even when they "wake up," they tend to deny the truth of what they are actually seeing. They go to great lengths of fantasy to distract their attention from the real facts of the matter, or to make unlikely excuses when all else fails them.

Like the professionally-hypnotized person, you tend to think thoughts or allow thoughts to surface only if they do not remind you of what you did "under the influence." Your ego is like a magnet, attracting only positive, complimentary ideas and rejecting all others. Such an attitude of rejection erects a barrier against the state of awareness.

Hypnosis affects your ordinary, conscious thinking, because your soul comes out of its compulsive experiences with all sorts of guilt and anxiety. Stained with sin, your soul now consciously repels truth, both in the spirit and in the thinking about it; it reaches back, beyond the hypnotic state, for the means to persuade other people to give you the delusion of reality you need if you are to preserve your prideful nature.

The waking state, then, is linked to the things you do in the hypnotic state. For that reason, you find yourself automatically rationalizing what you have been compelled to do, even after you are no longer under the influence of the hypnotic pressure. You can reject Truth when you are conscious, because you do have some sort of choice in the matter. To know the Truth or to reject it is the proclivity of the soul itself; so, depending on your attitude, you can descend to, or ascend from, the sleep of deception.

No doubt, you fled to the sleep state in the first place as the result of the first trauma you were not prepared to meet. The wicked stress drove you into a mild hypnotic state and made you afraid to come out, for fear that the stress you would encounter out in the world would only drive you back into your shell again.

How can pressure do this to you? The answer is simple: In your vanity, you render yourself inferior to every stress you are likely to encounter. Anyone or anything that is strong enough to make you aware of your fears and inferiorities is bound to upset you, because you can't bear to see those fears and inferiorities exposed. If you were not so addicted to maintaining a superior image of yourself, you could face the cruel stressor, who has been playing with your wimpy evasions like a cat with a mouse, and even call his bluff. You could ponder over the facts involved in the stressful situation, ask questions about what is not clear to you, and arrive at some workable solution, which might not necessarily be weighted in favor of your adversary. Instead, as long as you cling to your dream state, you elect to run from seeing the painful truth. The truth is painful to you for two reasons: one, you fear the exposure of guilts you are aware of, and two, you can't face the possibility of its exposing still deeper layers of guilt that you have refused to see at all.

Your inability to bear the truth challenges your proud ego to suppress your awareness of fear, to get rid of it entirely, so you flee to the sanctuary of your imagination. There, you find relief from the awareness of fear and inferiority, while you explore your unconscious mind for answers. You have inherited a proclivity for losing yourself in this fashion. It is the only way your ego has of eluding awareness of inferiority, and escaping the realization that you simply lack the objectivity and wisdom to cope with life.

You have been dealing with life hypnotically ever since you failed the test of your first trauma. It is the only ploy you have known how to use for protection from whatever is bigger and meaner than you are. If it hasn't turned you into a fierce monster with a chip on its shoulder, it has turned you into a weakling who almost *invites* the fierce ones of the world to step on it. (I am using the "it" words here deliberately, because the hypnotic way is certainly not the human way to go.)

The hypnotic state of mind takes a stronger grip on you with each succeeding stress because of the panic you feel as you struggle in vain to find answers on the mental level. As a result, you learn to lose awareness at the first sighting of stress, and to start fumbling around in your imagination for ways of feeling superior and "above it all," ways that exist only in your head. You know, but you really don't know, so you *think* you know, and that's all that matters to you.

Many years ago, while I was practicing hypnotic therapy, a young woman answered my ad for a secretary. Months later, she confessed that the only way she could get up the courage to come into my office and apply for work was by seeing me naked in her imagination. She felt compelled to "put me down" in that fashion in order to cope with what appeared to her to be my overbearing presence. It was the only way she could find to deal with the awe and fear I had unwittingly inspired in her.

If the stressor is not aware of his role as stressor, as I certainly was not in my first encounter with the secretary, or if he is ignorant of the psychological effect he is having on the stressee, the stressee is left to himself to come up with some unique solution to make the situation bearable. He "arms" his consciousness with it, and it thus becomes a habit pattern that may stay with him all his life.

Losers have millions of ways of "winning" in their own minds. They can see total capitulation, for instance, as a kind of "love" for the terrorists who have captured them. It isn't, of course. What it is is a means of placating the stress and changing the enemy into a friend in order to make him more manageable. It is an attempt to gain control over the enemy through cunning, or to lull him to sleep by a great show of "loyalty." After all, if you learn enough about the adversary, you might be able to get the shoe on the other foot and become a stress to *him*. Have you ever tried to speak up to someone who has succeeded in making you like him a lot? You can't. Because he has managed to *make* you into his friend, you can not be his enemy. He has hypnotized you into changing places with him. Now you are on the defensive, and he is off the hook.

A weak person will often try to capitalize on your own weakness, an inability to say "no" to his impossible demands, by insisting that you meet him at a certain place at a certain time, and then showing up late with some elaborate excuse, or not showing up at all. How often have you felt like kicking yourself for not having had the sense to say "no" to the distasteful arrangement in the first place? And have you seen how your own weakness opened the door to your friend's hypnotic suggestion? Or have you been too busy lambasting him for his inconsiderate behavior?

The underdog type of person is quick to catch on to the fact that being late is a surefire means of upsetting the person who is either lording it over him or is simply making him feel inferior without knowing he is doing it. In either case, being late almost always succeeds in upsetting the other person; so it becomes the manipulator's favorite way of dealing with people on his own level. It becomes such a habit that he might find it difficult to get to his own wedding on time.

Of course, there exists the rare person—the kind I would like to see develop as a result of my guidance—who fails to become upset at all. When the manipulator confronts this person, and fails to get an angry reaction, he is forced to face his own duplicity and feel the guilt of it.

Another scenario: The "perpetual latecomer" succeeds in upsetting his "victim" beyond his wildest dreams and opens the floodgates to such an angry deluge that he winds up in the loser's role again. In either case, the person who tries to use tardiness as a means of upsetting others can look forward to a growing fear of facing people as he becomes increasingly irresponsible and secretly contemptuous of those who are beating him at his own game, as well as those who are having the same effect on him through their innocence.

You must wake up to what is happening to you. You must discover the objective state of grace that will enable you to deal with stress properly. That is to say, you must acknowledge the Truth and remain conscious of the fears and inferiorities that are responsible for your various problems. Observe the problem before you, and acknowledge your own helplessness to deal with it, instead of running to your mind for answers. You might not see the power inherent in a simple change of attitude right now, but as you progress with meditation, you will understand its magic.

Now, to get back to the stressor-stressee relationships. If you look closely at what is going on in all your associations with the people around you, you will see that it is a constant battle for the "upper hand." You may discover that however much you scheme and plan to come out on top, you can never stand to face the guilt and fear such tactics arouse in you; so you give in to the demands of others and get to be known as a "good sport." You will develop false friendships with strong people, and no matter how much you may come to fear them, you will find it difficult, if not impossible to crawl out from under their control. From their point of view, you are so easy to "use" that they may become addicted to your services, even though they have little respect for the way you perform them. Some of them, on the other hand, may be completely taken in by your "friendships," and you *will* have the upper hand, but you may develop so much contempt for their gullibility that you will feel compelled to knock the props out from under them in some way. You are always trying to figure out in your mind some way to counteract the hypnotic stresses that continue to challenge you and find you wanting, unable to cope.

Government itself has to maintain its edge in the battle of upmanship by means of the pressures inherent in the political system itself and by keeping us aware of the threat to our safety that is posed by the possible invasion of a common enemy. If the people are not properly organized under their own system of stress, they can easily be taken over by an invading power. The aggressor then takes over where their own political system leaves off. You may not realize it, but any pressure, skillfully applied, is capable of converting you to its service. If you don't know how to resist pressures in such a way that you retain the upper hand, you will be dominated from all sides: religiously, politically, and personally.

Your reaction to stress controls you in two ways. First, it plunges you into the hypnotic state; then, it plants the suggestion that will direct your behavior. Without direction, you might become hopelessly confused by all the possibilities you can conjure up, none of which can offer much hope for a solution to your problem.

War is the strongest stress you are ever likely to face, for it affects everyone at the same time in the same way. In their fear, the people look to their political head as they normally do to their own mind for guidance. If the government then does guide them, the government retains its hold on the hypnotic reins of control. In return, you retain your cultural identity and intelligence. Otherwise, you would go through a political or religious conversion. War cures confusion in society in an intensely personal way, by uniting the vast, heterogeneous assortment of people under one absolute authority. When he sees how effectively stress can be managed by the government on a national scale, any common corrupter soon learns how to consolidate his power over his victims by arousing their defensiveness against someone that he suggests is their enemy. Usually, it is someone who poses no threat to them at all.

Stress is the means by which all suggestions gain control over you. The pressure flips you to one side or the other. Then, the threatening stress becomes the sustaining stress, and the source of your direction.

Life itself exerts a strong hypnotic influence over all of us. We all keep busy trying to influence one another, even as we all keep busy trying to throw off those influences. And it is the struggle, the hopeless battle itself, that prevents your functioning in a meaningful way and causes guilt and conflict for aggressor and victim alike.

By spotlighting this fact, bringing this basic truth up to your conscious mind for recognition, I hope to wake you from your lifelong trance.

4 Rebellion and Comformity

Once you have fallen into a trance, you never really wake up, partly, because you don't know how to go about it, and partly because you are afraid to see what has happened to you. You continue to live in a day-dream, recreating past scenes to improve on the role you played in them, and looking for answers, not in Reality, but in ever more "perfect" fantasies.

You respond hypnotically to every pressure. Either you rebel, or you conform. Or you might first rebel; then, finding you lack the confidence to put up a real fight, you give in and go along with the pressure. You start out one way, and end up another. Sometimes, we back off even though our first efforts at rebellion succeed in throwing the stressor off balance, simply because we fear the power that we hadn't known our resistance would give us, and we don't want to take responsibility for it. At this point, if someone comes along who is in sympathy with our "cause," and offers us his support, we might hand him the reins along with our services. We take from him the direction that we were afraid to take for ourselves. A young criminal often finds himself with a smoking gun in his hand, totally unaware of the skillful way the master criminal managed to place it there. He would rather take the "guilty" verdict than admit to being completely under the control of another person.

Similarly, we often fail to see any connection between the stupid things we find ourselves doing and the real stress that is driving us to do them. We burn the toast or get upset over the morning's news in order to work up enough energy to go to a hated job. We actually create little stresses in order to escape seeing our mishandling of the important stresses in our lives.

The guilt we accumulate as the result of trying to resist the suggestions that were laid on us early in life will drive us eventually to a life of "peace-at-any-price" conformity.

You have little reason to doubt that you are living in a trance state. It may be an organized or a free-floating trance; that is to say, one without immediate direction because of the rich variety of impulses that can set it off. In the latter case, you find yourself doing many disorganized stupid things, often asking yourself, "How did I ever get into *this* mess?" Most of us are wandering through life in this condition.

The organized zombie, on the other hand, is a person who takes his direction from one fairly specific source, a person or a system of belief to which he has pledged loyalty to the death. A good example of this is any one of the many persons who went to their death with Jim Jones in Guyana. When our minds fail to provide us with answers of our own, we tend to look to other people, and beyond them, to their governing spirit as it exists in various occult and esoteric practices.

Obviously, when you lose awareness, you lose

intelligent guidance. When that happens, you look to your imagination for guidance, and when that fails, you fall back on the expert manipulators—politicians, for instance—and the more you depend on them, the more you need them in order to function at all. Most of us are living on some "layer" of this hypnotic state, and we hit bottom by the time we die.

Every culture, simply because it sets itself apart from the vast commonality of human beings, exerts a mildly hypnotic social pressure on those who identify themselves with it. It is this pressure that accounts for the anxieties and fears of the cultural man or woman. Somehow, we seem to know, on some unplumbed level of understanding, that to be a cultural *anything*— a Jew, an Italian, an Englishman, a Nazi, or even a cannibal—is unnatural. You must yearn to be what you would have been, had society not messed around with your mind. Every person who identifies with a culture, or rebels against it, feels anxiety, because his conditioning, habit patterns, and prejudices conflict with reason. The conflict being waged in each member's inner being drives the entire society to distractions of all kinds. Each social order has its own kinds of drinks, drugs, dances, and diets that sustain the people's identification with the group.

I do not intend to dwell at length on the other forms of compulsive behavior, except to say that the hypnoidal state leads to all of them by virtue of the pain and fear it produces. The victim is always driven to remove his pain. Left to himself, he experiments; otherwise, still in his trance, he is led down the garden path to the permissible, tried, proven, and accepted

51

forms of pleasure. His trance state deepens as those unhealthy practices debilitate him physically.

Once in the trance state, which, incidentally, often does not seem much different from the aware state, the ego may become afraid to wake up, to know the truth. It turns to stimulants, like coffee, tea, tobacco, and drugs, for the emotional energy to keep awareness at bay. In that sense, drugs are hypnotic, as well as analgesic. The truly natural way to be is *fully conscious*. Left to himself, a person who has been hypnotized will come out of his trance unaided, provided that he has not been made to do something immoral or degrading; in that case, he might want to stay in his trance so badly that he will fake a conscious state on being told to wake up.

Drug addiction, alcoholism, and criminal actions are trance-inspired, for the most part. The shame of compulsive behavior, whether induced by conformity or rebellion, seeks relief in the pleasurable practices that reduce a man's consciousness of what is controlling him.

You are probably not aware of the role hypnosis is playing in your own life, but take a good look at your reactions under stress, or in anticipation of a danger or pressure that is bigger than you are. Watch what happens the next time you know you must stand up to your boss or your child's teacher. The very thought of it causes your heart to race and throws you into a panic. There you are, back in your hypnotic state. The mere expectation of danger triggers a hypnotic condition that duplicates your response to the actual stress. You take refuge in the dream scenes that are typical of every person who has ever lived to realize his inadequacy. You escape the truth concerning your vulnerable and uncertain state by reaching down into your mind, where you can find the only answers you know about, where you exist yourself, secure in that knowing. Do you see now how the ego solves the problem of awareness of fear, ignorance, and inferiority? In the hypnoidal state, your ego is less aware, even somewhat secure—somewhere down there, you think there are answers you can call your own.

The very thought of facing stress throws you into a hypnotic state of anxiety. The mind races for answers, while your ego escapes from seeing its fear. But getting lost in a sea of thought does not solve the problem of guilt or fear; it actually increases it. Because you fail to cope again, you weaken your ability to become consciously aware again, you are more afraid to face the Truth than you were the time before, or the time before that. You need the awareness-reducing hypnotic presence of "friends," and even of enemies. You can never trust zombie friends, no matter how personable they are, because they can transfer their allegiance to other causes, other friends, at any moment.

Perhaps, down there in your worry, an answer will hatch out, and on a sudden impulse, you will become violent. Maybe some silly verbal reply that does not fit the situation will pop out to brand you a bigger fool than ever. You antagonize friend and enemy alike, as you scamper back to your dream state. So you can stay in your mind, too frightened to move or to do anything at all. So you don't. The mild form of this terror is called procrastination. Another form of procrastination results from not having enough stress-motivated energy or hypnotic direction to move.

If you fail to come up with a satisfying answer of your own, the impatient person, to whom you have given authority by virtue of your reaction to his stress, will invariably force you to go his way. Soon, you develop a habit pattern of not being able to function until someone screams at you.

You might marry someone who substitutes for an overbearing parent image. You do this unconsciously, almost hypnotically, partly in order to keep functioning in the identity that has been established in you, and partly to avoid the anxiety you associate with being fully aware.

You can relieve anxiety in either of two ways. You can dive into a deeper "sleep" by moving away from reality into a "sense" of innocence, or you can move up toward the Light, repent of your ways, and become truly innocent, at one with your Parent Self.

Let's look at some of the methods manipulators use to put us into the hypnotic state (in case we are not already in it):

TERROR: If you have read the preceding pages, you know what a powerful force terror is, and how easily it can be used to control you.

SEDUCTION: When you flatter someone and build up his image of himself, he is all too glad to discard the anxiety that has been eating at him for some "unexplainable" reason, and come down to accept the lovely ego-image you offer him. Now, he won't look back; he becomes addicted to approval and flattering images, and will sell himself down the river to get them. Any anxiety his hunger might wake in him only forces him to keep on serving his flatterer to maintain the hypnotic effect on which he has built his security.

AMBITION, WILLFULNESS: An ambitious, willful person is easily tempted, if you know what he wants, and are able to hold it, or the hope of getting it, *just beyond his reach*. At this point, when his greed is almost palpable, it's hard to say whether it would be more effective to deliver what you have promised or to withhold it. A promise, once fulfilled, stirs up a little anxiety, a little question, "Is there more where that came from?" But a frustrated ambition will also cause the victim to try harder, and go along with other schemes and plans you might offer him, because he is afraid to wake up as a greater failure than he was before you seduced him. If he were to see his foolishness in its true dimensions, he would have to admit to the superiority of his deceiver. So, win or lose, he must cling to the deceiver to reinforce the "rightness" of the original ambition and to remain unconscious of how he is being used.

Would you like to see how the principle works? Just ask a strong-willed friend to clasp his hands together and concentrate with all the willpower he has. If he knows how to exert will, he will follow the suggestion as you continue to repeat it, until finally, when you tell him that he can't open his hands, he will be unable to do so. He is hypnotized. Anyone who is too ambitious, who tries too hard, who studies too hard, gets lost in his imagination, so lost that he can't get back again. He can go insane or he can even commit suicide. Do you see how evil gets our attention and eggs us on to the bitter end?

Here is another experiment: Get a person to visualize

a beautiful scene, and when he has developed a vivid picture in his mind, ask him to step into it. Lo and behold, he gets locked in his imagination and is unable to come back to consciousness until you command him to do so. He has been hypnotized.

The professional hypnotist rarely uses, nor does he really need, fancy gimmicks, like crystal balls or swinging pendulums. He applies the force of his overbearing manner. That is all he needs. If he is a doctor, he may offer you a cure, or promise to help you uncover some great, untapped power of the mind. He controls you by driving your ego into its imagination, where you will accept a cure without realizing why.

A salesman will often use a joke to create a hypnotic shock. Any extreme of comedy or drama, a sudden change from one mood to another, will do the trick. People can't cope with change. It throws them into a trance-like state that is hardly recognizable as such, but they become more manageable as a result of the shock. People joke all the time as a way of dealing with stress and making a friend out of the enemy. We gladly yield to the hypnotic effect of tragedy and comedy on stage and film as a respite from our own problems and suffering.

EST: A concentration-camp, gestapo-like approach. It is amazing to think that a person would pay good money to be totally brainwashed and humiliated, but that is the treatment he will get from EST if he is desperate enough to turn to EST for an answer to his problems. I refer to EST here because of the thoroughness of its approach. It is so thorough that it is able to completely rebuild a man after a few days of intense indoctrination. The man is let out into the world again with a brand new personality, but that personality is still locked into its creator, Mr. Erhart.

Basically, the technique is to strip the individual of all familiar crutches, such as family and friends. A number of strangers are locked together for a bizarre and expensive weekend. Each one in turn becomes a victim as he is forcibly humiliated before the others. Then, when he hits bottom, his breaking point, he is suddenly applauded and accepted by the crowd. I understand that, in the meantime, he has not even been allowed to go to the toilet and has thus been forced to wet his pants. If so, the brainwashers are going all the way back to early toilet conditioning in order to get in on the ground floor and do a proper job.

One reason forced humiliation works so well is that it so closely duplicates true humility, in which repentance is followed by change and then by the acceptance of the parent spirit: becoming a nothing-so-something-can-be sort of thing. We have all tried being a big something and have wound up a big nothing, so we figure it wouldn't hurt to try turning things around the other way. But what if we misconstrue the mystical meaning of humility, and continue in a downward progression in order to become a new person? The Devil himself will challenge us to play that game with him! So when being brought low becomes a means of getting high, what you have is an extraordinary form of possession, a hypnosis of the kind that Hitler used on his Nazi followers.

Whenever your ego has schemed and planned itself into a terrible guilt, and when all the knowledge and talents you have acquired in order to accomplish your goal cause you more anxiety than they cure, when the identity you have acquired and sustained by means of all those supports becomes unbearable, it is time to seek salvation. Just remember that there are two kinds of salvation, and when the ego is stubborn, it converts humiliation into a virtue. When the newly conditioned man is freed from his old self with its trailing conscience, he becomes a new creature with a new chance, a new lease on the same old life of vainglory.

You see, the pain of humiliation, of becoming a nothing, is bearable only because it closely resembles the yielding associated with the true repentance that produces meaningful change. How gladly you strip yourself of everything you associate with the old man, the former self. How happy you are to strip away the old knowledge and replace it with a new system of words, slogans, and hypnosis-inducing habits. No suffering is too much for you to bear, knowing as you do that you will step out later in a completely made-over identity, with less consciousness (no conscience at all), and with access to many new ways to go on your guilt-free, merry way.

Even religious verses and chapters, repeated mindlessly without understanding, will cause hypnosis. They, too, will produce a form of religious behavior without really changing the troubled person who is going through the motions. If a charismatic Christian does not smoke or drink, it is only because he does not need to, inasmuch as he is already high on what he thinks of as his Jesus.

For the most part, it is the music and religious phrases that displace the compulsive agony of scheming, planning, and worrying, and give you the illusion of salvation, of having solved the problems of anxiety, failure, and just not being able to cope. As long as you are given a chant by a friend, who is really an enemy, and there is some form of positive direction coming up through the chant, you can not worry, and you don't have to see how rotten you still are. Order has overcome confusion, and you think you are religious. You chant along with the rest of them, supposing yourself to be "praying unceasingly." In time, you become too paralyzed to take on any meaningful work. You become addicted to the enemies in friends' clothing, because you need their presence to save you from seeing yourself and feeling guilty about what you see.

THE MANTRA: A word chanted over and over again, designed to focus the mind and relieve it of guilt. Hare Krishna is a good example of hypnosis, brainwashing, and conditioning combined, because it leads the individual into a totally new and structured environment. Each new symbol, food, exercise, or gesture holds a post-hypnotic key to link the cult member to the one experience that "saved" him from his former way of life. These cultists are fanatics, slaves, zombies—almost without hope—unless you can isolate them forcibly from the group long enough to remove the post-hypnotic suggestions of the words and conditions that keep them locked in a trance state.

THE MEANINGLESS WORD MANTRA: You might think that the meaningless word mantra is harmless because it appears not to be loaded with the suggestions you fear. But it is far from harmless. Suggestions often work best when they are implied, rather than spoken. Suggestion leads to worship, so much so that the mantra meditator winds up worshipping a deity without being able to see that that is what he is doing. TM claims that it is not a religion, but it is, even though the hard-nosed, anti-religious businessman or politician fails to see that he is caught in that trap. Whatever frees you from conscience, whether in a wrong way or a right way, *is* religion. And in this world of deception, religions exist that are simply very subtle forms of devil worship.

People relate to inference and symbolism better than they do to words because the symbol represents a mystical "something" that cannot be seen. And that happens to be the way the human soul was structured to respond from the beginning. It was *meant* to translate the unseen into the visible and tangible in thought, word, and deed.

Dictators rely heavily on symbols for their profound meanings, and their ability to effect greater changes in behavior patterns than words can. A good symbol, into which you can read meaning, has a basic root that flowers out to become an elaborate system of thoughts, either maniacal or heavenly, depending on its source—symbols like the swastika or the cross of Christ. The mind was designed to elaborate on an implanted mystery, so that a total personality grows up from the symbol in the heart. Your implanted mystery makes you read meanings into things that may, or may not, be there.

If you look carefully, then, you will see that the meaningless word is not so meaningless after all. People are word-oriented. They have been painfully deceived and misled by word manipulation. They are afraid of all words; yet they need direction. Some of us are even afraid of honest, meaningful words, because they tend to awaken in us the pain of conscience. Enter the specifically-designed, meaningless word mantra! You can lose yourself in it so easily, and *voila!* instant relief! Like magic, instant salvation. The mind is no longer in a state of confusion, rebellion, or conformity. Here is a new sound that inspires the soul to innocence, that triggers no memories. Nothing comes with it to lie to you, and nothing comes to wake you. But it does carry the implication that you are alright the way you are. Your problem disappears because all you can hear is the meaningless word, and you lose yourself in it as you float away from reality in a trance. Confusion gives way to peace and happiness. You no longer have to tempt guilt by monitoring your vain goals, because the guru, or his duly authorized agent, is in control. The love and reverence you feel is a growing need that you think of as love.

The hypnotic trance state is restful (only if it is controlled by an outside operator) because, by its nature, it smooths out conflicts and mental suggestions, thus saving you the energy you used to expend on fighting your impulses. The mantra you were given preoccupies and smooths out the mind, which had been running away with itself, exhausting its energies by having to come up with answers. What could be more refreshing?

No person will smoke or drink under structured hypnosis. Why? Simply because, in that state, he does not require drink, smoke, food, or drugs, by reason of the fact that the state he is in takes the place of the other things and has the same effect on him. Hypnosis effectively reduces the conflict that used to drive you to stimulants, both by removing awareness of the problem and by distracting you with another presence (the hypnotist). So you are happy for awhile, but hypnosis has a diminishing return. You have to find new ways of reinforcing it through people, drugs, religion, music, etc.

As long as you are locked into your meaningless word, of course, you cannot see that you are hypnotized. You can not see what your guru, the master hypnotist, is up to, because the excitement of his presence and the meaninglessness of the word preclude your being able to understand anything at all. At the same time, the gratefulness you feel toward your guru makes you want to please him, and you think of your worship as love. You think nothing of kissing his feet, if that's all it takes to succeed without guilt. Later, after your initiation, all you need to throw you back into your restful trance state is "the word." A word is a thought, you see: a thought that can conjure up the image of one who can throw you into a state of panic, or of infinite calm.

All you know is peace, joy, relief from an inhibiting conscience, freedom to go on, to take the forbidden route without a trace of guilt. But the link to your guru is always there. This link is known as "rapport" among the hypnotic elite.

What saves you claims you, so you had better be sure that what saves you is God, the Parent Spirit of Conscience, Who silently testifies to these words about the deceiver of the world and the angels of hell who do his bidding.

5 The Hypnosis of Love

By now, the reader is probably aware that one of the most powerful, wordless forms of hypnosis is induced by "love" and acceptance. Those who love you as you are exert the pressure that *makes* you what you are, from the beginning to the end. This is an immutable law. It works both for good and for evil, depending on the source.

Cruelty evokes an emotional reaction, the pain of which causes you to give in. The pressure may be sudden and strong, or it may be applied persistently over a long period of time and lead to a nervous breakdown. The buildup of cruel pressure, skillfully applied, will cause you either to conform to the pressure source or rebel against it. If you happen to conform, you might (and might not) be greeted by acceptance, in which case your tormentor changes roles and becomes an ally, a newfound source of support, who will promptly use all the energy you once expended on resistance to further his own ends.

When you begin to feel a physical need for the life support that entered your consciousness by way of shock, you think of it as love in order to reinforce the new identity it has given you and to gain the energy to function. This reaction explains why *instant acceptance* (love, to you) is such a powerful form of motivation, whether you are on the giving or the receiving end. It also explains why you are never happy with what you do or what you have.

Again, I repeat, *those who "love" you as you are represent the stress that made you what you are.* Every friend you meet carries within him the original stress that is also the enemy. Friends are really enemies in disguise, accepting and manipulating your changing nature to serve them. To understand this truth is to lay bare the power of the female mystique and of your friendly used-car dealer.

The presence of the enemy in the role of friend still carries the hypnotic escape and motivational value it had when he was your enemy. Although the pain of enemy presence changes to pleasant feeling after you have conformed and adapted, it is still something of a shocking pleasure you experience in the company of phony and vile people. You are so completely taken in by those who accept you as you are that you will practically dive into them, like a sea lion dives into the ocean, to escape seeing the truth of what you have become. And the lower you sink, the more rotten you become, the more power these lowlifes will have over you.

The shock of any form of cruelty triggers a compulsive, hypnotic state of mind that makes you eager to please your friends. Obeying them, you are becoming more like them, and you are ceasing to be yourself. The shame of doing wrong things in order to please others may drive you back into the hypnotized state for escape, but there is where you will end up having to please them again. When you escape Reality, you wind up in the same state of mind you were in when you fell under the compulsion to commit the sin in the first place. In this condition, you need the presence of violence or the acceptance of violence as a friend; this need feels like love for the person who is able to relieve you of pain and guilt by keeping your ego asleep and falsely secure. You see, the state of mind you were in when you did not realize you were doing wrong is the state of mind you return to in order not to see that you are still doing wrong. It is also the state of mind that causes you to see your enemy as an understanding friend who loves you.

For this reason, you always return to the scene of the crime—in marriage, in business, in so-called friendships. We are all drawn to the familiar spirits that made us what we are: a woman's husband becomes the father, or even the mother, she hated, a person she thinks she loves only because her need draws her to him. In the presence of our seducers, and for the sake of their presence, we do wicked things. When you are with them, your ego experiences a false emotional security as you use them to reinforce your corrupt physical nature. It can be one hell of a delight.

Do you see why it is so pleasant to sin? Every sinful act actually involves two pleasures that seem like one. First, there is the delight of escaping from the confines of the "enemy" conscience. And at the same time, your fallen self gets its earthy refreshment as your stupid ego experiences the delights of distraction. The release from inhibition creates a false sense of innocence; you feel shriven. The presence of the despicable friend or enemy helps you to grow and come alive in a more degenerate way as it relieves your anxiety over the last time you came together, and it eases you down another notch.

Friends, like the guileful women they are, for the most part, will seem to serve and surrender to us as a means of weakening and conquering us. They do it in order to change places with us, to get our identity and authority. People whose own true identity and authority have been displaced will do unto you what was done unto them. The inferior nature of the corrupter changes places with the victim and dominates him with seductive ways and pretentious services.

To hypnotize you and take his place as your authority, all any scoundrel need do is play the familiar game of love or violence, or both at the same time. That is, he pressures you mercilessly until you yield, and then he turns on the charm and can't do enough for you. Your craving for acceptance has a great deal to do with your not having had enough support for the identity you were developing during your formative years. You may have had wicked parents, who rejected you and totally denied you love as a means of commanding your services. The ego's craving for love always inclines toward pleasing wicked people. You really believe that your godlike love (need) for them will eventually create in them an answering love toward you. Don't you see how the implanted Hell in you keeps trying to command the services of the Hell that created it? Can you see why other hellions might be afraid to love you? They will be more likely to compel you to serve them their private Hell by rejecting you the way your parents did. The more you try to get them to serve/love you, the more you will end up serving them.

When you fail to find fulfillment, you will become so hateful that you will become like your parents with your own children. You will try to fulfill yourself through them by using them as your parents used you. And the reason you are so desperate for love is that, in your vanity, you equate fulfilled need with salvation.

To succeed with you, every manipulating friend must have an enemy core concealed by the plastic exterior, simply because it is the enemy factor that offers the hypnotic escape, "service with a smile," as well as the physiological support you crave.

The enemy presence literally overwhelms you, so that you lose your own thoughts, good ones along with the bad ones. You look only for assurances, verbal and nonverbal. You find the nonverbal assurance in the form of the hypnotic personality's shock presence. Now, the stage is set for various verbal assurances— directions, suggestions, lies, and praises that your ego, in its lost state, craves to hear.

I can safely say that, without exception, your misguided love for others represents your need to run away from yourself, or from someone else's hypnotic grasp. Until now, it has been the only means you knew how to use in your fight against reality. It was your egocentric way of making a new and better life for yourself. But where did it always get you? Out of the frying pan, into the fire! Divorce, anyone?

Man's psychophysical need for a guileful female can

be traced back to original sin, our common heritage, the original hypnosis, creator of physical change and the awareness of it. Modern man has inherited an unconscious need for the presence of the woman who changed him from a real, eternal man—which Adam was—to the violent, or whimpering, woman-worshipping, unprincipled male beast he is today. Tempted by the man's need for her total support, every woman "lovingly" rises to accept the ages-old role of hypnotist, which she inherited from Eve. Or was it the snake? However she came by it, she has an inherent knowledge of how to entertain and sustain male illusions of grandeur. Today's Eve soon discovers the terrible motivational power within her psyche that her poor degenerating brute can neither see nor understand. Soon, the little wiles that served their relationship so lovingly in the beginning grow to monstrous proportions and overpower both of them. Eve doesn't know how to stop acting the way she has been programmed to act, and Adam just feels trapped. He responds by rebelling, running away to another Eve, or by throwing in the sponge and becoming a super-lover of a merciless, liberty-taking wife.

Until man finds true love, men and women are destined to be chained together in unholy union, the woman clinging to the man for his earthy life and power, and the man using the woman's presence to reinforce the hypnosis of his pride, along with the mortal animal nature that is born of pride, as he falls ever more deeply asleep to Reality.

The male ego's need for a female to play the hypnotist's role is as pressing today as it has ever been during its long run in the cycle of tragedy. Dictators "love" people and people "love" their "female" dictators. We see here a case of mutual abuse. Tyrants love the weakness of the people for the sake of the power it gives them, and the vast masses of people love the deception (hypnosis) that is practiced on them by those to whom they have given power. It follows that when people become thoroughly degenerate, they will dig up dictators out of Hell and bestow upon them the power to rule the world with their peculiar madness. How gladly do the utterly demoralized souls accept the exquisite tortures inflicted upon them by the damned of their own making and choosing. So it is with the ego of man; he brings tragedy down about his ears through the very woman he craves—and elects to power.

Throughout your life, you will be experiencing one, or both, of these two forms of "love," and in all your involvements with other people, you will either control or be controlled. You may evolve to become like the devil who passed his corruption on to you during your formative years. And when you take on the mantle of that type of personality, you will feel the security and power that inheres in the pressure source. You will then allow others to use you, to bask in your divine, hypnotic presence. You will let them revel and renew themselves in your presence in exchange for the power they are giving you to control them. If you are a man playing this role, be advised that you are playing a part that is typically female, surrendering in order to exact surrender. When you forsake God for woman, you take on her nature. Think about it.

Instant acceptance sets the stage. The shock of love

at first sight, or friendship at first sight, is irresistible; it is without doubt the most basic form of hypnosis and corruption in the world. It is used, not only by women to catch and control their men, but by the Madison Avenue gang, the priestcraft, and other despots whose sole aim is to gain some kind of control over us.

What you get in the process of being violated or accepted is a kind of mirror image that tempts you to complete it, to make of it the reflection of a new, and false, identity. In order to do so, of course, you must give up something of your real self, and as you do, the impostor cries out in you to be fulfilled, to take over the newly-created vacuum that nature abhors, and fill it with violence or with violent love experiences. You begin to experience a great anxiety that drives you to seek escape from the old self in order to "find" yourself in the new experiences. While you busy yourself with escaping Truth on a psychological level, you are also reinforcing the false, vile, sensual self on the earthy plane. If, on the other hand, you are the violator, your reward for playing the role of hypnotist and tempting your victim with the glorious image of himself you have planted in him, is his very guts. You draw up the life essence of your victim to power the false demon self that is growing up inside you. The victim gets his "something missing," which keeps crying out to you for its completion, and you get the power that you think you need for your own completion, and the more you get, the more you want.

For God's sake, watch out for those "nice," plastic people who just love to put their paws all over you with gestures of affection. Beware, also, of the violent types who drain you while stamping you with "their" identity. Evil tempts, both with "love" and with violence.

Always be on guard against the "lover of the world," who sees no evil in anyone, who loves all the people in the world "just as they are." These "lovers" are more deadly than vipers. They are men who have exchanged their identity with their mothers and are now obliged to play mama's role by coddling the sinful, violent nature of others and helping them grow to serve "mama" in daddy's body. A frightening percentage of successful leaders—businessmen, ministers, politicians, professional men—are latent or overt homosexuals.

Watch out for the parents who see no evil in their wicked children, children they have brought into existence and spoiled rotten in order to serve the Hell that was planted in them by their own parents. Remember how Hitler himself was "born" into existence as the bizarre brainchild of the wretched German people. He could never have gone it alone on his own power. Innocent eyes would have seen him as the madman he was. When virtue runs out, evil rushes in to take its place.

People who love you as you are always evoke the spirit of some bygone trauma. The corrupting evil is always traumatic. Its nature is overtly or secretly violent, and under its hypnotic spell, your seducer feeds you the missing bits that you crave for your new identity. As you mature, you become more and more like your corrupter (even a dog will grow to resemble his master), and you will tempt others as you were tempted, away from their true identity.

Perhaps we should not find it so strange that we grow to look at wicked people as good people, once we have been trained to capitulate to them. After the inital indoctrination, our egos refuse to believe that evil is evil because we enjoy the illusory benefits of its presence inside us. We find it hard to believe that the godfather evil, which understands and sustains its identity within us, is evil. It is far easier for us to believe that there is something wrong with the good people, because their presence pains us by threatening to wake us up. Aware people do not encourage you to continue in your hypnotic trance. They tear down your illusions and threaten your whole wrong way of life.

The way of life we develop as the result of falling to the temptation of our worldly lovers compels us to seek out villains to serve us. We even put them on pedestals, and sometimes we see them as our personal saviors. Sometimes, you might even see the villain coming and seduce him into being your friend before he has a chance to upset and dominate you. As a friend, enemy core notwithstanding, he can sometimes be manipulated to serve and sustain the ego/animal nature you have inherited. All the naughty ego games we play with one another exist for the sole purpose of keeping us asleep to the Satan-loving hypocrisy that controls us all.

Remember, if you happen to meet up with any of those see-no-evil, hear-no-evil people, and you fail to challenge their perceptions, you may be placing yourself in danger of letting them turn you into another Hitler.

Do you see now why people crave an environment of war and violence on one hand, and the blandishments of their hypocritical leaders on the other? Violence and intrigue fulfill and complete us, using the same techniques false love uses to perform the same service.

Do you also see why children are fascinated by monsters and scary bizarre things? Monsters distract and excite their little minds; they help them grow up to be ego animals. Indeed, I see this phenomenon as a normal part of human ego development on the road to maturity.

Everyone inherits a fallen, ego/animal nature that must be allowed to grow up with gently correcting love until it is mature enough to bear truly supportive love. If that nature is never corrected at all, is always loved "just the way it is," it is robbed of the vital *repentance* experience, and the spoiled brat grows up to become a wicked adult. If you love a thief *as* a thief, he becomes *more* of a thief. We all have secret weaknesses that grow worse when they are "mothered" by the people around us, who see them as engaging personality traits. We even brag about them, as: "Oh, he knows better than to mess with me and my short fuse!" You must learn to rebuke others, that is, make them aware of what they are doing, with love (patience without judgment) before you will be able to love them with divine, truly redemptive love.

Wanton love causes more conflict than it cures. For one thing, it intensifies your resentment of the friend who is lavishing it on you, and soon your resentment makes you feel guilty. Finally, the guilt feelings drive you to need the love more than ever. You dare not speak up for fear of losing the ground of your false being, the identity you have taken on as the result of looking at yourself in all the lying mirrors. You are drawn to your violators for the security you feel in their presence, and you lose sight of the vile nature that is growing inside you. You may finally rebel, but then what happens? Your "lover" will either become violent and incite an answering violence in you, or he will decide that he hasn't loved you enough and will offer you more of the sweets that have already soured in you. So you love him back hatefully, or just plain hate him back. And feeling guilty about it—back in the ring you go. You can not free yourself from this hypnosis. All you can hope for is to get the "upper hand" and become the hypnotist/bully/tempter/tyrant/seducer yourself.

The wrong way of life has disqualified you from having the natural grace to stand up against evil. Your prideful, corrupt nature needs and wantonly loves the evils that are creating and supporting it. How can you oppose them? Where would you be if the world suddenly became perfect?

Let's take another look at the way people are able to take advantage of the identity that has been projected into you by your parents. Needless to say, the identity they have passed on to you is the one that was projected into them by their own parents, and they were compelled to pass it on as a way of getting back at the evil that brought them into existence. Unfortunately, or perhaps fortunately, the ability to create a subservient hellion does not always guarantee the dominance of the creator, because the child (or friend) who emerges may grow to dominate the life out of its creator, either with syrupy sweetness or mean violence. Parents frequently become their children's children, to be "shown off," and worshipped, or kicked around and blamed for everything. In trying to command Hell to serve them, ignorant parents end up recreating the identity of their own parents (already alive in themselves) in their offspring.

Here is a classic example: A man gets away from a "sweet" little dominating mother and marries a woman who seems to be submissive—certainly, not dominating—who loves him as he is (the way mama created him). For a season, he feels like a creator whose divine love (need) has drawn into existence the exact kind of woman he needed to complete him—that is, to hypnotize him into compliant ecstasy. But sooner or later, the day will come when all of a sudden his mother shows up in his wife. What a shock!

Men are constantly running from one woman to another, violently or lovingly trying to find dominance over the indomitable spirit that continues to dominate them. In the process, they often become mamas themselves. There is no escape. The same guileful spirit of mama must be in every woman to sustain what mama has made and to keep it hypnotized. And if he accidentally happens to be drawn to a guileless woman, his craven need for the serpent in the woman will drive him to draw it up from her dark side, or even try to project it onto her if the woman nature in himself is strong enough to conjure it up in all its subtlety. In the process, "he" winds up loving himself in "her," and the roles become reversed. The woman becomes the man who serves, and the womanly man holds the hypnotic reins of power.

Humanitarian "goodness"—loving and being loved—is a game people play with one another to feed their egos. The kind of goodness we see in hypnotized people comes from a weakness, from a firmly established habit of yielding to dominant personalities. If you are one of those persons, and there is no evil eye around to furnish you with that kind of hypnotic security, you go out and find one.

So-called primitive natives employ many strange rituals to keep away evil spirits. Yet if you look carefully, you will see that what they take to be the "evil spirit" is their own conscience. All the chants, fire dances, ceremonial masks, bead rubbing, and candle lighting antics have been concocted by tribal witch doctors to provide their victims with the hypnotic security they need for their stupid, degenerate egos. And the power stays with the chief.

Once a thought has been established in your mind through the shock of pressure, that thought, all by itself, can stimulate the same hypnotic reaction in you as the presence of the person who used the shock to get to you. When you relive past love/hate scenes with people, you are able to re-create the hypnotic states your ego needs in order to escape reality and ease anxiety feelings. As the romantic memories rise to the surface, so do the strong, nostalgic love feelings. You allow your consciousness to float along on these fantasy-created "good" feelings in order to escape bad thoughts and feelings. Everything associated with your nostalgia has a turn-on value for you: a lock of hair, a handkerchief, "our song,"—all these incidentals give a power assist to the high you are so desperately pursuing down memory lane.

On the other hand, all you have to do is *think* about your enemy, and up jumps resentment. But remember that resentment is not only hypnotic; it feeds the ego with judgment. All forms of hostility stimulate a high that can help a person forget how wrong he has become as the result of resenting his enemy. The enemy's presence was hypnotic, but to dwell continually on the mental image you have of him is to reinforce *his* nature in yourself. You grow high on judgment, even as the thought of your "lover" (enemy) caused you to grow high on ecstasy. Either way, you are getting away from your true Self.

You may be a willing, or an unwilling, victim of dangerous posthypnotic teases. Images of the past, acting as a real presence, constantly relive themselves in your mind to cause conflict and compulsive behavior. Everyone around you has inherited mannerisms that excite and reinforce the compulsive love and rebellion patterns that took over your consciousness during your formative years.

For a season, you can use one love/hate fantasy after another to tease yourself into a trance state. The false security you derive from the hypnotic state and the images it evokes become the only reality you care to know, offering, as it does, such total freedom from anxiety. So, for a while, you live down in your mind with false happiness, security, and freedom. But to keep the trance state fresh and exciting, you have to keep reinforcing it with music, drugs, and new experiences that produce new fantasies. The deeper emotional states of hypnosis produce the most vivid dream visions and the most inviting escape from having to face the repercussions from previous escapes. But there *are* repercussions. As long as there is a spark of life left in your conscience, the hounds of heaven are hot on your heels and threatening your precious illusions. You must either give up, or run ever faster toward your music, your pagan rites, and your rotten friends.

It is not in the nature of things for any "high" to last forever—what goes up comes down. And as the energy level of excitement goes down, boredom sets in. And boredom is painful, because it has a way of draining the life out of illusions and forcing your ego to wake up to reality. Like a primitive aborigine, you become terrified by your aloneness and by the falseness of what you see in yourself. You are bored, "fixed" in an empty time frame, too afraid and too guilty to go on using people and things for your narcissistic delights. You have used up all that was "on hand," and you are too drained to scan the horizon. This is the bottom, the blessed time for those whose destiny is graced by a call to salvation, because they were too preoccupied by their excitements to hear that call before.

But those who are determined to go the way of corruption will blunder through the shallows, seeking new adventures on lower levels, with ever more shocking friends and comforters. Corruption builds the prideful nature on the ecstasy of the trance state. New adventures will bring new compensations, new impressions to entertain as the old memories entertained—just before they became the tortures of Hell. Watch the facial expressions of musicians, their eyes rolled back in their bloated sockets, as they enjoy the mental orgasms of their trance. Look also at the silly grins of entranced music lovers.

There is a sameness about all the living patterns that

lead to death. In all the time that excitement is producing its carefree illusions of freedom and forgetfulness of life's true purpose, the corrupt self grows more ugly and vicious, more craven in its need for still more excitement. (It has been said that music tames the savage beast, but let me be the first to tell you that it also makes the beast more savage.) It is now the sick, displaced self, the ugly caricature of the Self that was meant to be, who cries out for ever more disgusting experiences with which to renew itself and escape the truth of what it has become. Unable to resist the cravings of its degenerating base nature, your ego submits to one false salvation (hypnotic involvement) after another, each one contributing its bit toward the renewal of the bestial life—the only life you can know as long as you live in a state of unawareness.

Remember that people can control you through objects. Anything associated with your fall from grace can take you over completely; it can have the same effect on you as the corrupter's personal presence. Any object that you took note of during the traumatic experience has the power to affect your behavior hypnotically. In controlled hypnotic procedures, the hypnotist often plants a posthypnotic suggestion in the subject's mind, sometimes simply to prove to the subject that he *was* indeed hypnotized, and sometimes simply to save time in future sessions. In doing so, he transfers his authority, his control over the subject's mind to some object (a magazine on the table, perhaps) or action (a snap of the fingers, a handshake) by suggesting that the next time the subject encounters that object or action, he will find himself back in the trance state. It is a highly successful technique, perhaps because we are so hungry for direction from the powers over us. In the absence of a direct suggestion from a hypnotist, we will tend to grab on to anything connected with any traumatic stress situation to carry us back to it.

The same principle might explain your tendency to overeat. It could be that whenever your mother saw that she had upset you, she might have tried to pacify her guilt by cooking your favorite dish for dinner, tempting you to have another helping, and basking in your enjoyment of her artistry. Isn't it strange how mother's food always tastes the best, even when it isn't? Then, there are the folks who must chew every morsel of food a hundred times before they swallow it. Could it be that they are just trying to prolong the hypnotic effect of the food? The health-book arguments they use to justify their habit are nothing but handy rationalizations.

Some excellent examples of object excitement are the erotic feelings produced by the sight and feel of ladies' lingerie, and the effect of a religious symbol, like a cross or a string of beads, on the person who has just undergone a false conversion. Giving a string of beads, or an amulet, the posthypnotic power to produce a trance state provides the victim with a handy way to relieve himself of his guilts, anxieties, and conflicts. Rubbing the beads reduces the convert's awareness as it produces the feelings he associates with salvation.

Sex, religion, politics, drugs—all can be used to chase away demons and promise a renewal of life, a kind of salvation. Don't misunderstand me. I don't mean to imply that there is no such thing as true salvation. All I aim to do here is to expose the kind of salvation that is mass-produced hypnotically by the spirit of deceit after it has captured its victim under false pretenses. The presence of Evil *saves* you only in the sense that it *saves* you from seeing what it has done to you. Your ego grows addicted to your "friend" for the false comfort and "values" he brings into your life. Your fear of God makes you more vulnerable to the suggestions of the tempter, whom you feel you must obey in order to know salvation. But the sinful things you do for his approval drive you back to needing his presence for comfort.

Hypnosis, as well as posthypnotic suggestion, works in either of two ways, either through the rebellion, or the conformity syndrome. Each is reinforced by the personalities or symbols we meet as we go through life.

Take the example of the son of a rich man who hates his father, and everything associated with him—especially the money that is so dear to the older man. The boy grows up to be a bum, rejecting money as a symbol of evil. He tries to be good by doing the opposite of everything he thinks of as bad, like making a lot of money. He bases his whole existence on a mindless rebellion against his father's values. All his life, he keeps reexperiencing his hatred by rebelling against money and anything else his father values. His suffering is enhanced when he notices that, in spite of all his efforts to be different, he is beginning to resemble his father—as he surely *is*, because hate cultivates the seed that hate has planted. Now, he may marry a woman who seems to be the exact opposite of the witchy mother who always supported the errors of his hated father. But what he gets is support for a rebellious, egotistical way of life, and through that support, his father's nature takes shape in him despite his piety and his rejection of worldly values. The poor man's wife is like his mother because she supports his ego in its wrong. As his pride grows fat, his guilt and insecurity might even drive him to become the kind of success he hates his father for being.

Let us suppose that another son of the same rich, corrupt father is a conformist; he surrenders so completely to his father's values that he, also, bases his feeling of security on the hypnotic lure of money. He loves the presence of money in the same way that he loves the presence of his father; so he marries a woman just like his mother. One way or another, the dynasty goes on.

The boy who comes from a poor home, if he is a conformist, may completely resign himself to being poor all his life. Poverty represents his righteousness and hypnotic security. The rebel son, on the other hand, turns his back on poverty and looks for his security to the objects that support his rebellion against it. He might achieve financial success, but money produces as false a security for this son as poverty did for the son who resigned himself to it. It makes little difference what those objects of security are. They all work the same way. They all contain posthypnotic triggers to keep the victim in line, chained to his miserable drive to fail or to succeed. The only way out of this hell is to wake up to reality.

The anxiety caused by never knowing where the next meal is coming from drives the poor man to look for more assurances than poverty can provide, and the priestcraft is all too happy to leap into the breach with its hypnotic techniques of salvation, helping the poor to sink still deeper while renewing their faith in the goodness and righteousness of poverty.

The rich son's rituals revolve around celebrations and rewards, not because he has achieved anything of real value, but because partying blinds him to his failure to achieve. He might even give large sums of money to "positive-thinking" churches to justify and sustain him in his glorious greed and guilt. Succeeding is as compulsive as failing, and the hypnosis of it drives men to be as rich/miserable and church dependent as the poor man is poor/miserable and church dependent.

The poor man finds solace in wine, women, song, and drugs just like the rich man, because they are just the same inside. One is a poor, degenerate slob, and the other is a rich, degenerate slob, and as they hate each other, the rich man becomes a richer, more brutal drunk, while the poor man becomes a poorer, more brutal drunk. Their shared compulsiveness keeps them going in their chosen directions.

The presence of the corrupter is so powerfully hypnotic that you can never react to him in a common-sense way. Your human reason is paralyzed in his presence. No matter what you have planned, it disappears down the drain when your corrupter, your friend or your enemy, appears. His mind and will become your mind and will, and whether you like it or not, you begin to identify with your enemy as enemy or friend. If you totally conform, you become like him inside and out; if you rebel, you become on the outside what he is on the inside. Your compulsion to conform or rebel is reinforced in the presence of those in whom you see a familiar spirit.

You can't really rebel against the system, because the act of rebellion is the projection of Hell that converts you to the service of Hell's purpose on earth. In your rebellion, as in your conformity, you are on your way to becoming what the evil in the stressor wants you to be. As a rebel, you are just as guilty of not being yourself as the conformist is. As a rebel, you are drawn away from the obviously rotten conditions that spawned you, toward something that looks more honest, but your obviously violent nature will need the obviously violent presence to sustain you in your rebellion. You will use the hypocrisy of others, as in the case of the two brothers, to sustain you in "righteousness" and reduce your awareness of what has gone wrong with you.

Obviously wicked people will find other wicked people to love them for their beautiful wickedness, just as hypocrites attract the wantonness of other hypocrites. To satisfy your love of hatred, you will do battle openly, but underneath, you are two of a kind.

Are you a person who just loves to make people happy? Do you bend over backward to please? If so, you are weak. Your only idea of goodness has been to give in to the pressure of others. Or you may have the goodness of the manipulator who knows how to elicit and make use of the apparent goodness of others.

Few of us are able to live without pressuring or being pressured, so out we go to pressure or to get pressured. You may be so needful of pressure to get going that you might imagine people are pressuring you

84

(your boss, for instance) when it's the furthest thing from their minds. You can make any object play the motivator's role. You can hate your work to gain the motivation to escape from it, or you can love it for the motivation to escape into it.

Remember the rule. Objects may assume a people/ spirit role, especially objects associated with the original corruption. Women's underclothes can produce erotic feelings because, for a man, they represent a female extension of his mother's body presence as it has endured in his consciousness from infancy. Clothes, because they "stand in" for a person's actual presence, can influence, arouse, and seduce the person whose yearning has given them the power to do so.

If you have read this far, you probably see that you are not in command of your own life, and at the very least, you would like to be able to shuck off some of the world's conditioning and start the journey back to the Self that you were born to be. For starters, stay alert and aware. Become conscious of the things that you are responding to, and observe the reason for your response if you can see it. You might not be able to do this 100 percent of the time, because your emotions will be pulling the other way, making you less conscious of the moment. In fact, it is the emotion, the wrong response, that should concern you more than the thing that triggers it. If you were totally objective, you would not be reacting to anything with emotion and would therefore have no need of rationalizations and excuses. No doubt, the first wrong reaction you see in yourself will be *resentment*. Then, if you are a sincere searcher, guilt feelings will set in, and depending on the strength (or shallowness) of your commitment, you will be tempted to seek distraction in still other feelings for escape. Or you might even enjoy wallowing in the guilt feelings, in the faint hope that your *mea culpas* can evoke the sympathy of those you have wronged. When we doubt that God can forgive us, we look to our false gods for forgiveness and comfort. Watch it! You don't want to be a masochist all your life.

Men, do you see how dangerous it is for you to react with impatience toward your wife? Only a weak person who needs the enemy for sustaining love will get caught in that pattern of behavior. Men are always being defeated by their love and their hate, and women are always frustrated by the unmanliness of men who fail to conquer them with patience and self-control.

Very prideful, willful people respond very badly to honest correction. That is to say, instead of welcoming the correction, they resent seeing their egos exposed, and it matters little to them that the correction was not an act of deliberate provocation. When the proud one feels victimized by such a correction, he may go through a stage of *false remorse,* composed of emotional pain, self-pity, and guilt, a morbid sadness over having been defeated and exposed. To relieve the pain, he gives in and serves to get approval and support for the corrector's identity that is evolving within himself. This is the standard technique a guileful person uses to rise from a position of subjection to absolute dominance.

All conquered, resentful people are treacherous indeed, serving those who conquer or expose them only until they can find a way to turn the tables and conquer the conqueror.

Observe your relationship with your employees, your spouse, your children. See how important it is to stand as a contrast to their emotionality, forbearing to add fresh impetus to it by being impatient with them. See clearly why you should not be upset or impatient with others, especially with your children. You should not even be too eager to accept them when they please you. Your impatience makes them wrong, and your acceptance serves and supports that wrong. Never be too close, too loving, with *anyone*, lest you turn him into a weakling monster. Be neutral, kind, firm. Remember that impatience is hypnotic.

6 The Power of Deception

Corrupted persons—criminals, for example—grant their first loyalty to the powers that have made them what they are, and they stoutly resist any attempt to correct them. Because they see any such attempt at correction as their mortal enemy, they greet each succeeding attempt with a greater resistance.

If you have ever experienced the hell of having a child come home "different"—changed by some away-from-home-experience—and if you have suffered through endless frustrations in your attempts to set him straight, you had better pay careful attention to what I am about to take up with you. First of all, you must arm yourself with calmness and patience; then, you must be strong enough to keep that child from his friends, their music, and other activities they have been enjoying together. You must give him time to survive his withdrawal pains and come to his senses. Be careful here, for if you let him off the hook too soon, he may be tempted to think he has just won a round in a battle of wills with you. Above all, you must always be sure that you yourself are not exerting a wrong kind of influence over your child, and to succeed in your efforts, you will do well to familiarize yourself with the psycho-physiology of corruption. As a mature adult, you have no parent to hold you back, other than the Parent-Self consciousness that alone can set you free.

Let's pull aside the veil over certain animal relationships for a moment to see how the principles of dominance and submission work.

In nature, the leader of the pack or the herd is the one to whom all the others submit as the result of having been beaten by the leader or of having known better than to challenge an obvious superior. Of course, the losers identify with the dominant animal, usually but not always a male, and thus preserve the unity and safety of the group by following the leader and developing their own skills against the day that they might feel up to challenging the leader and becoming leaders themselves, with full procreative privileges. Until such a time, they are *compelled* to identify and follow, simply because anything that threatens the leader is a threat to the entire pack. This is the principle of identification, a strong cohesive force that is shared by man and beast. In the case of man, however, this writer contends that a tendency to identify oneself with dominant personalities is the result of an inner failure that allows dominant sinners to take charge of all us lesser sinners and make our lives a misery until we find a way to get the upper hand, or, better still, find the Truth that sets us free from the dog-eat-dog system of things.

In the natural world of lower animals, it is usually the male who fights and dominates other males, but in our human world, it is the woman who has cast her shadow over failing men from the beginning, so that men who are driven by ambition for leadership end by becoming more female than male as the result of their lifetime devotion to, and identification with, the power behind the woman.

What works well to produce order in the animal scheme of things throws confusion into the descending man as he struggles to assume human leadership. The failing soul, you see, cannot stop with its own body identity, or its identification with "glorious" superstars, heroes, and giants, because shame is always catching up with him. He is compelled to lose and resurrect himself in a never-ending cycle of identification with one great leader after another.

Homosexual behavior can be produced in laboratory mice simply by overpopulating their living space. The hostility created by the pressure of overcrowding forces the males to react to females as they normally do to one another. In due course, they become so imprinted with the female identity that they begin to act like females.

Have you noticed how men have been affected by their war with the dominant females in their lives? Their proud egos identify first with the female body, then with the female herself, and later with female-oriented male heroes—all this in an attempt to escape the shame of what they are becoming in the mysterious process that has claimed them. Female-imprinted males enjoy the company of other males and indulge in hero worship of macho sports personalities in an attempt to regain their lost manhood; but that is what it remains: an attempt.

By separating the soul of man from his true ground of being, temptation introduces into the psyche the physical stress factor that causes change; and as long as man's ego is unwilling to face the truth of the weakness responsible for the change, he will remain subject to pressure conditions that will continue to alter him. It is this phenomenon of the kind of corruption that results from environmental conditioning that this text explores and exposes.

Each time you are overwhelmed by a dominant personality, each time you give in, something of the identity of the conqueror slips inside you and begins to develop pridefully as it demands support.

The trouble is that in your vanity you tend to compensate with animal submission as a means of either becoming or conquering. Through various forms of hero worship and putting people on pedestals, you find it is possible to win the conqueror's love, which you use to support the conqueror's very own nature inside yourself. If you were to carry this process to its ultimate conclusion, you would weaken your hero by completely gobbling up his identity.

In psychological jargon, we are speaking here of projection and transference. Exchanging identities and swapping roles are all too common between man and wife and between mothers and children, especially when the child is a son. Strangely enough, the principal cause is too much of the wrong kind of love between the conqueror and the conquered.

Remember the dark rule, which is: Those who love you as you are embody the temptation that made you what you are. We become the projection of the intelligence that lurks deep down inside the people who "mother/father" us into children of darkness. It is particularly the influence of the mother pressure that accounts for the hell we know on earth. I use the term "mother/father" to describe that invisible, destructive, seductive, and supportive (you can do no wrong) love that has its roots in the nature of woman and comes to flower in her offspring, from one generation to the next.

The loving, reassuring "mother" presence is hypnotic; but more than that, her ego-sustaining love is a powerful motivating force, one that every vain man demands her to supply. Motivating mother-love must be distracting and exciting; otherwise, it would fail to transfer or reinforce the false identity that awaits us in the security of the hypnotic dream state. So the motivation and the "love" that make a person forget one thing (Truth) and cling to another (the false identity) are really one and the same thing.

Let me run through that principle again: A woman's presence is magnetic, exciting, and hypnotic. It is also pleasurable, thanks to the pain-relieving effect of distraction/motivation. The chain reaction that begins with excitement looks like love, because it reinforces what men think of as manhood and pride of ambition. In other words, through the distracting, pleasurable, motivating, sustaining power of hypnotic love comes the identity of the source, complete with a plan and the energy to carry it out.

Lost in its hypnotic conditioning, the soul of man has exactly the same relationship with evil as the one it should have with God. The craven ego/physical *need* to remain asleep in the ground of his corrupted being is, to the fallen man, love for all that is holy. The identity of the female, secretly growing up in him, sets the stage for an actual identity exchange to occur; whether or not it does depends upon the individual's power to compensate and to repress.

Worldly love is the reinforcement we crave for what has gone wrong with us. It is the medium through which is projected the netherworld identity that, sooner or later, identifies itself as us, and sometimes even dares to openly declare itself to be God. This type of thing represents the principle of identity projection; carried to its limit, it results in total exchange. Man serves the evil in the person who has conquered him in order to become the god that each personified temptation *is*, in its dark, negative sense. In some mysterious way, women have conquered men, and men now worship women in order to experience conquest at close quarters. They do so in order to regain their lost power and identity; but men, devoid of understanding, are like compulsive gamblers, sending good money after bad in the attempt to get their money back.

As the inherited Eve-mother-sown identity flowers into malehood, the earthy, sinful ego-self begins to cry out for stronger reinforcement than the ordinary wife's love can provide. If I have just described the way you have evolved as a man, you unconsciously *demand* that the partner you are using, and falsely believe you are conquering, sink lower and lower in order to excite and satisfy your ego needs. Angry and dissatisfied, you go out in search of whores, immoral high priests on various levels of hell, who are already devolved, unconflicted, and obligingly degenerate. With the scum of the earth, you experience new shock-engendered escape from reality and relief of anxiety feelings, followed by a sustaining love for the more craven, loathsome self you have become. For a little while, you may be content to think of that corrupt, base, sensuous, vile, unprincipled, cruel, unruly self as the real you, but it is not the self you were born to be.

False love, like true love, comes from an intelligent source, and carries with it some of the identity of that source, which seeks to express and project itself into the world.

For you, there are *two* sources of sustaining love, and, depending on your inclination, your soul will accept, embody, and manifest one of these spirit sources. Whichever you choose, real love or fake love, you will undergo a creative or molding process. Through hypnotic deception, fake love, you lose true life and identity in exchange for a false life and a corrupt, subhuman identity, while through God's sustaining love, and His presence within you, you abandon the death identity in favor of life eternal.

Only through realizing God's indwelling, abiding love, can you experience an exorcism of the love for, and from, evil. You will also find that His realized Presence is a great motivating power. Through your awakening consciousness, His Presence will manifest and project through your person. His Presence will expose and devastate the evil identity, and for those willing souls you meet along the way, you will find that you have the power to awaken them and set them free.

The Creator's Presence is ever available for you to realize as you rise in consciousness from the various depths of hypnosis into which you may have fallen. You feel His correcting Presence as you allow yourself to realize the errors of your former way. A tingle of embarrassment will quicken your nerves like fire to burn out the old identity and its old ways. Alas, for those vain and stubborn people who try to resist the Light in you; they will feel the fire without the purifying change.

Let me speak more about the negative side of the positive life, inasmuch as that is the side you know best and are thus most likely to understand.

Bear in mind that, as a seeker, you may stumble on to the flip side of the negative process of transference when you are naturally drawn to a more highly evolved seeker, who is also a teacher—as you might be to me; but until this time, you have been developing your false identity through a series of transfers from one authority to another. First, you had your friends; then, marriage; then, the other woman; then, drugs? drink? the priestcraft? the doctor? the witch doctor? By the time you reach the mortician, you are ready for the "heaven" of hell. The evil identity in you, craving completion, has been drawn to people of rank who have tempted you to seek fulfillment through experience.

The process of transference, wherein you are handed over to lower personalities for programming, is too complex and multifaceted to chart on paper, but the various stages will sort themselves out for you as your consciousness clears through meditation. Here are some classic examples to jog your awareness and get you started on the road to a more complete understanding:

If you are a power-packed personality yourself, there could well be a time when you pushed your victim so hard that he rebelled; thus, you lost your friend or lover to another powerful personality or system—a church, perhaps. From there, he may have gone on to drink, and from drink, he might have gone back to the church, or he might have lost himself to both at the same time.

Or perhaps you were the victim of a pushy personality, and after the one push too many, you transferred your allegiance to an exciting new religious figure, or a lover, who had the power to lead you hypnotically away from the previous enslavement.

An ambitious woman can push too hard and end up losing her husband, not only to other women, but to a fixation on success, on drink, or on all three of them together.

You could even experience transference of an authority's identity to yourself. An eager-beaver worker can act so much like the boss that he finally becomes the boss, and he may even take off with the boss's wife.

A married man may crow like a cock one moment, and cackle like a hen the next. The mother-smothered son becomes a homosexual.

People often identify with their pets, and even come to look like them after using them as objects of worship. The sick often identify themselves with scientific progress so much that after several operations, they feel superior and "more advanced" than the well ones outside the charmed circle of "progress" and medical breakthroughs.

There are those who use the principle of submission to produce a kind of false deliverance and religious behavior; but evil, working from its hidden abode, is pulling the strings.

In our hypnotized, zombie state, we are all authority-

and personality-prone, actually giving up power to others as we transfer identification from object to object, from hero to hero. We actively seek identification with an "ultimate truth," even if it turns out to be the devil himself.

Guileful men know full well that you demand escape through hypnotic identification, and knowing which identity it is that you are seeking—namely, God's—they can proclaim themselves to be God, knowing that many of you will throw yourselves at their feet, hoping to attain identification with the leader, God, through your idolatry. But what actually happens is that *they* become *you*, because the real you will have ceased to exist. Remember what Jesus said concerning this type of thing. He admonished the people of his time not to accept those who came in their own name of glory, while rejecting him who comes in God's name.

To this day, at the lowest point in mankind's slide so far, we see the "beautiful" people, the grand, glorious gods of entertainment, the music personalities, greeting the degenerate masses with instant acceptance and identification, in order to let the poor fools identify with the god before whom they prostrate themselves. The guru from the pit can look like a genuinely religious person, or like an ignoble rat, like Hitler; either way, the effect is always the same. You become an evil that thinks he is good, or an evil that is never bad, because when you attain to the evil godhead, evil is god, and god is never wrong.

The hypnotic curse we all live under is a legacy from long ago, from the ego of the first man, who, aspiring to the Godhead, fell from grace under the hypnotic spell of a beguiled Eve. Within the framework of his woman-orientation, modern man is tantalized to pursue the indwelling female evil as the ultimate good, to inherit death as part of life. Until we learn the lesson of pride, we are delivered up to the wicked shepherd.

Every hypnotic involvement changes you by degrees into the likeness of the intelligence that lurks behind the glorious objects of distraction and worship, until one day you seem to become the object of worship yourself. No doubt about it, you can so completely identify with whoever it is that he takes you over and runs your life until you become him. Should you manage to escape the ravages of insanity, disease, and tragedy, you might eventually personify Satan himself.

Pressure and Identity Exchange: Some of the Results

Homosexuality:
One of the most obvious results, of course, but we have already examined this aberration in previous pages.

Murder:
It is not unusual for a young man to harbor murderous thoughts against his mother. He can become so enraged and rebellious against his mother's indwelling, dominant evil that he can begin to see murder as his only solution, the only possible way in which he can hope to salvage whatever is left of his selfhood. He sees himself becoming like the mother he hates, and frustrated by his inability to stop the process, he allows his rage to build up until it erupts and drives him to the

ultimate act of violence: murder.

Of course, the desire to do violence to another person is not so rare that we haven't all felt it at some time to some degree, but we learn to let it out in less harmful ways. We compensate by judging, or lording it over, our adversary, or we take it out on ourselves by getting sick. One thing is certain: until we learn to deal with our wrong reaction to pressure, it is bound to manifest itself in some way. The hypochondriac may simply be a person who is desperately searching for a "jailer" to prevent him from giving in to his violent, anti-social rage. Taking to his bed and letting everyone wait on him is his safety valve.

But once a person has cultivated his killer instinct to a high degree, he might find himself lying in wait to catch his intended victim in a defenseless or weak position. He might see his mother sitting quietly in a chair, and be seized with the impulse to kill her. The hell that has been growing up inside him as the result of his mother's pressure has always been a coward, subject to the shaping presence of the dominating authority, answering it obediently while growing in its likeness. Now, the time comes when the spirit of the monster in the mother completes itself in the son, and he turns the tables, reverses the roles, and if nothing intervenes, kills her. The Frankenstein spirit of the mother is destroyed by the monster it created in the son. The Queen is dead. Long live the King.

Murderous and strange sexual thoughts are often directed toward mother substitutes, women who resemble mother in some way. The reason for this is that, until the corrupt nature is fully completed in the likeness of the hell that is creating it, it dare not turn its fury against its maker—after all, it is still dependent upon it for its existence. Until it has grown to its full potential for evil, it must sharpen its skills on easier prey. Incidentally, this explains why soldiers rarely kill the browbeating sergeants who are trying to make "men" out of them. The sergeant is a mother substitute, so it's prudent for the soldier to direct his hostility toward the *enemy's* mother and *her* boys.

Men will sometimes dress up in women's clothes in an effort to possess mama's identity, to become whole, complete, and possibly even independent of mother. This is especially true if the man happens to have murdered his mother, or if his mother or his wife has died. Out of guilt, he tries to bring his mother back to life. He takes on her identity, and reinforces it by wearing feminine garments of the most personal and seductive kind.

Fear of Heights:

If you have a habit of yielding to pressure, you may feel drawn to throw yourself off a tall building, simply because that is your established way of reacting to pressure. Something of yourself has been drawn into the pressure source, even as it has been drawn into you. When you stand on a high place, you will see yourself conforming to whatever it is that the danger scene seems to want from you. And of course, what Evil or danger always wants from you is death. Its stress draws you in the direction of death, and you play with morbid ideas about killing yourself. A rebel makes a good steeplejack because of his absolute refusal to conform to pressure.

Hoplophobia:

This is a fear of weapons, especially firearms. This condition appears most often in a person with a displaced murderous identity. Such a person's first impulse, in the presence of a gun, is the urge to kill with it; but because he suppresses the urge immediately, he interprets his reaction to be fear. (Of course, it's possible that some fear is actually involved here, because he has had a narrow escape—if the urge to kill had hung around longer, he might have given in to it, and we often experience a delayed fear reaction after a narrow escape.) Some people acknowledge their fear of guns openly; others ascribe their reaction to some religious fetish, or simply say, "I am above that sort of thing," meaning anything to do with violence. As a rule, these people feel godly, and secure in the belief that if they never own a gun, they will never find themselves in a position where a gun would come in handy. However we want to look at it, a fear of guns has everything to do with how we see ourselves using them; we fear them because we know that situations could arise in which we would be all too glad to use them, and we don't even want to think of the consequences that might result from a wrong decision to do so. How would you like to be the rookie policeman who killed the little boy because he thought the toy gun was real?

The recognition of our human propensity to kill that lies behind one person's fear of guns is shared by the person who is fascinated by guns and may even collect them, but in his case, he is confident of his ability to make the right judgment in any given situation. At least, he has no need to rationalize his interest in guns.

The Fear of Signing One's Name:
The victim of this relatively uncommon phobia cannot sign his name because he is no longer himself. In most cases, he is unaware that anything is wrong with him until he goes to sign his name. At that point, he feels that the familiar name represents someone else entirely. He no longer relates to it at all. "Who am I?" he wonders, and he is overcome by fear.

Every ego trip has as its objective, knowingly or unknowingly, the attainment of the Godhead by the ego making the trip. For this reason, the most powerful words anyone can utter are those that endow the hearer with the key to a power that can make all his dreams come true and send him in pursuit of the forbidden fruit.

Such words caused Snow White to eat the apple and fall into a deathlike sleep, from which only the kiss of Prince Charming could awaken her. Surely, this fascinating story, told in fantasy about fantasy, evokes the memory of Adam and Eve. Man, too, has fallen asleep in a living death, and he awaits the divine Presence, the Prince of Peace, to wake him from his trance. But listen! *His Presence is within you now, testifying to the words on this page.*

Appeal to the ego works as powerful a magic today as it did in the beginning, when Adam fell asleep to the beautiful Reality he had known through God's Presence in Paradise, and wakened in the jungle hell of his ambition.

You have no need to take my word for it. Just wake up, look around, be aware, and you will see all sorts of snakes in the grass, promising you power and deliverance. "You can have what you want to have; you can be what you want to be. Power and riches can be yours..." And then you discover what you must buy, do, or work for, and you find yourself serving the ego-builder for the promised advantage, until it dawns on you that there *is no advantage*. The only advantage belongs to the fiend who holds up the illusive promise of advantage to others, that they may die to the dream he has them caught up in. Even if you were to outwit the dream merchant and compel him to make good on his promises (not that he could!), you would no longer be your Self. You would be made over in the image of the tempter. You would be the evil tempter personified, casting his hell over the earth.

It staggers the imagination to see the lengths to which people will go, the lies they will believe in, the depths they will stoop to, in the name of "getting ahead." And see how proudly they try to cover the symptoms of their failing with their tawdry "gains."

Take a good look around you, and you will see what it is that sick people and drug users want from medicines and drugs. They call it a "high," but it's a prescription from hell, an escape from seeing the harsh reality of their failure to be a god in the real world—it's the stubborn ego's last desperate bid for the Godhead in the illusionary world of drugs and medicines. Medicine must share the guilt along with the illegal drugs, because it, too, preserves the pride of man by removing his awareness, along with the symptoms, of failure.

The appeal to logic in the serpent's deception is as powerful today as it was in the Garden. To paraphrase, he said, "God knows you won't die. How can you die if the forbidden fruit makes you a god with the power to judge good and evil? Gods can't die. A god can't be wrong, can he?" Excuses! Excuses! The logic is false. We're gods all right, but only in our imagination, and we are dying. We can't see past our imagination to know the truth about the evil deception.

The object of the female-imprinted tempter is still the same: to become the god of what she sets up to be god, to make people into mindless zombies of an evil purpose, to have power over self-righteous sinners through the delights and hypnotic distractions to be found in objects of desire and deliverance.

Appeal to a man's ego, and you have him where he lives. He has inherited an ego that leans toward pride, and it is particularly subject to all those subtle pressures that sow and nourish his pride in achievement.

But once again, remember the dark rule: Once you have been tempted (pressured), you are a slave to temptation (pressure). You will find that this fact holds true of every temptation you encounter as long as you live. You have come into this world with an inherited proclivity to respond to evil pressure pridefully. Pressures that motivate us to be selfish and prideful lead us to exert the same pressure on others. The delusions of culture become our lord, and they lord it over us in no uncertain terms, until we grow to maturity and lord it over others, and those "others," alas, are usually our poor kids.

An appalling majority of souls see nothing wrong

with the system of self-glorification, of resignation to death (heaven, to them) as part of life. But some of us—the true children of Light—find ourselves in a desperate predicament. We can't enjoy our hate/proud feelings, we can't find joy in our wantonness, nor can we lose ourselves completely in the love/hate relationships that are so dear to the worldly ego.

The worldly and the unworldly alike—all of us—have something against the system of hell we live under; but the ambitious egos hate only the fact that they don't know how to "beat" the system. They rebel against the system, not because it is wrong, but in order to work up the energy to somehow evolve and *become* the very power they hate. Both the hatred, and the love that grows out of it as the result of the ambitious involvement, fire up an evolutionary pattern of growth that will continue on its unmerry way until we wake up to true love. Both hate and the adulterated emotion we *call* "love" are simply two horns on the same goat.

Certainly, even the children of the Light know what it is to hate, and thus open the door to the fiendish identities that are growing up inside us and making us just like those we hate. This is our dilemma. How do we resist without becoming like what we hate? Fortunately, the answer is simple. All we have to do is realize that to go on loving hate, as we tend to do, is to stoke the fires of ambition and contribute to the godless evolution of pride on earth, and, for us, that is not the way to go. We can hardly take a good, long objective look at the error of our ways without coming to repent of them; after that, because repentance washes away pride so thoroughly, we will be free to express our honest disagreement with the ways of hell on earth, and so separate ourselves from the common fate. We must not think we are wrong because we see evil as it is. The only reason for guilt is to *resent* the evil we see, because it is resentment that allows the evil to get inside us.

There are two ways of looking at perfection—or two concepts of it: the ego sense of perfection, and perfection itself. When one is not reaching for the ultimate perfection, for God, then one is unconsciously reaching to *be* God; and that kind of reaching separates us from the power that would bring us to perfection in the perfect way.

In our supreme folly, we try to make our prideful, imperfect self perfect. We work to become a wrong that is always right, a wicked self that is never evil in its own eyes. We do this, partly through the hypnotic process of escaping Reality and partly through identification.

Men are naturally taken in by the beauty of a woman. The worship of beauty is falling man's way of making up for the loss of beauty and goodness within himself. They worship the she-conqueror in order to obtain her power—but little does the victim know what will become of him in the exchange. He doesn't know that the values and power he sees in a woman are actually the strength he is losing to her, and his attempts to recover his strength serve only to make her more powerful.

By inheritance, a female is naturally superior—and therefore, a threat to a man. So it is only natural for a fallen man to fall even further for an attractive woman in order to acquire what he feels to be the missing part of himself. On the second leg of his ego trip, he even loses his male identity and gains a false one, much to his dismay.

So does man begin his slow journey toward death, always looking outside himself for what is missing inside. The more he gains, the more he loses the very thing he is seeking. The lure of beautiful people, and even the not-so-beautiful, becomes more and more irresistible to all of us. By now, the reason should be clear. It is simply that our tempters know the secret of how to take away from those who are drawn to them the very things they seem to be offering—life, health, riches, and honor. It drains you the same way gambling drains you. The more you lose, the more you bet in the attempt to get even, and the more you lose. The house gets richer, and you get poorer. You can't win. The richer the house gets (thanks to losers), the more it tempts and excites you to cash in on your fellow losers. You've been had, and your only recourse is to change places with what got you: the house, the deceiver, the woman, the devil, whatever.

Remember the rule: Losers, the defeated ones—sinners, in other words—associate with, in order to compete with, the identity of those who are lording it over them with money, power, riches, authority, or even piety. One way or another, they feel challenged to drink in the identity of those tempters, to become what they are. Wicked tempters are rich and powerful "kings," who get others to die to them even as they themselves have died to evil. They have nothing real to offer, only a flimflam, a pretense, a show, a carnival act they put on in order to satisfy the escape/identification needs of their glory-hungry victims. They have the guile to turn the sinner's stupidity into power for themselves. The hero worshipper, who makes the grade and becomes the hero himself, may now be rich, but he is also closer to hell, more tormented than his followers could possibly imagine him to be. Inside that tinsel personality, he is a monster, in unbelievable conflict as he secretly feeds on those he is tempting to be like him.

Attractive, well-endowed, beautiful people often develop problems that are never apparent to their admirers, in spite of the fact that it is the admirers who cause the problems with their adulation. The beautiful people find themselves in possession of a parasitic power to manipulate others that they don't understand. They even fear it. They may live in ease, but they are surrounded by treachery. Sometimes, they become so drained by their followers that they die of a massive heart attack. Actually, the idolaters, the "bleacher bums," secretly hate their inferiority to those they worship, and they enjoy seeing their heroes fall on their faces. The armchair fan loses himself in the ecstasy of identification with his favorite football player, but when his hero gets clobbered or makes a mistake, he can turn around and get just as much pleasure out of judging and blaming his erstwhile idol.

You would do well to remember the basic rule of temptation, which is: Whenever you see that someone has something you want for yourself, you tend to submit to that person's authority in order to obtain it. It matters little what that something is: sex, money, respect, a degree, a position, anything at all, as long as it's what you want. The powers that be will always control you through your greed. While you never really gain from them, you may learn enough from being around them to become like them and take advantage of others. Some of these exchange relationships are so subtle that you never see them taking place, while others are quite apparent, such as the identity exchange that takes place between man and wife.

The identity crisis is the biggest problem in the world today. People are always seeking to belong, to identify with someone or something, just about *anything* that will help to control them and channel their energies.

The urge to identify is so strong that just seeing a fellow human being, or even a lower animal, in an attitude of submissive worship, will tempt some people to "join in," and thus share their "godship." Does this not explain the pathetic idolatry of primitive people, the insane persons who think they are cats and dogs, those who think they are Napoleon, those who murder in the name of God or Jesus Christ—even those who claim to be pawns of the devil or the devil himself?

Taking drugs is a religious ritual, both of escape and of identification. Drugs make men feel good, and a good feeling is a God feeling. Therefore, drug pushers, high priests of drug religions, ministering their "blessings" to their damned, are that much closer to Hell than the damned they serve.

Rituals are designed to hypnotize the worshipper into identifying himself with the religion that created them. Church rituals seem to bring the worshipper closer to the god with which he wants to identify. Certainly, all who worship as a means of escape are secretly worshipping themselves. In so doing, they experience the secret ecstasy of all false religiosity. In hypnotic prayer, they become transfigured into the very holy object of their worship.

Let us remember here that the Lord God commanded Abraham to see that his altar was made only of rough stone. He did so because human artistry has a way of perverting true worship, enlarging the sin of pride, and introducing all the devilish turn-on values we have been dealing with in this chapter.

If you had been the first man on earth, the first to make the choice between obeying God and being God, your choice would no doubt have been the same as Adam's, and it would have altered your state of consciousness. Your decision would have lowered the vibration level of your consciousness to permit the transgression, the sin-self, to enter, trailing death and filling your mind with delusion. You could hardly have failed to notice such a change in your nature, especially in the physical nature for which you had traded your spiritual identification with the will of the Creator. You would have known the shame Adam knew when he saw, for the first time, that he was naked. Nakedness had meant nothing to him as long as his faith was in God, but now that he believed the serpent, it made all the difference in the world. Surely, you know the self-consciousness and shame Adam felt, for you have inherited it, along with the legacy of death as part of life, and the subservience to the dominant power of evil in our mortal nature that we refer to, quite correctly, as the result of having been born in sin.

Man's basic problem is pride, and the way it manifests itself in his relationships with women, particularly mother and wife. Women inherit a strong rapport with man's ego as well as his body, and a man's mother is often the biggest sinner he will encounter in his lifetime. All she has to do to stake her claim over him is to stimulate his ego or pressure him in some way—and from that time on, he is her obedient servant, her slave. All our emotional needs give evidence of our obedience to evil's hypnotic call to the pride that we have inherited as part of original sin. Our unwillingness to face that truth, our defensiveness, only adds to the evidence that our pride is hardening itself against reality, seeking security in something called doubt.

Covering shame with excuses, clothes, and booze, Adam's progeny continue to doubt the truth that there is something wrong with them. They continue to react compulsively, and they can't figure out why they are mysteriously growing more ashamed as they sink further in consciousness. We are that progeny; and at each new low point, we experience guilt in its least recognizable and lowest form: anxiety. It makes us feel as though we are being hotly pursued by an evil, vengeful spirit, but it is a distant echo of the voice in the Garden. We must run from it, cover ourselves with anything we can grab from the world, until we finally find relief in the escape of death.

At first, our ego escapes into its own imagination; later, it identifies with its body, and as it loses itself in the various appetites of the body, it has no awareness of the fact that it is sinning, none whatsoever. But down there in the dark world of sensuous pleasure, the serpent waits to corrupt us further, to arouse new appetites and the changes they produce in us. If a little

light should get through to beckon us back to innocence, he simply makes us change our beliefs and
doubt the truth of our wrongness, as he alters our
senses and habituates them to serve his hellish scheme.

That is the tragedy of man as we have enacted it
from then until now, and the only way you can save
yourself from the hypnotic power of sin and death is to
face Reality and repent of pride.

The fascination a man feels for a seductive woman is
both hypnotic and animal-magnetic. In a woman's
presence, a man is relieved of the anxiety he would
otherwise feel over the effect she has on him; he loses
sight of what the hell in her is reducing him to. Lost in
her, he doubts the truth of his failing, he dreams, and
finally "wakes" to a life of glorious potential. In his hypnotic state, he believes only lies and has no use for
truth, much less a belief in it, and he fails to see that he
is being eaten alive by an invisible monster. He loves
the woman one minute, and fights her the next, but he
can never win, because he is a born loser, too blinded
and beaten to fathom his legacy of tragedy. In frustration, he often turns to violence, murder, or war.

By now, you can probably intuit the other side of the
equation for yourself. You may be able to see why
guileful females are excited by vile, brutish men.
"Weak," submissive, female types of men excite the
larceny in women. The mere presence of a weak man
spells "easy pickin's" to a guileful woman, and makes
her feel secure, beautiful, and "in charge." She feels
the way a con man feels in the presence of an easy
mark. Of course, the excitement felt by these tempters
is different from the excitement of the victim, who is

drooling over the delights that are being lavished upon him so generously. Little does the victim realize that the flow of energy, the ecstasy, he feels in his mesmerized state, is an *outward* flow of his life force; in no way is it the fulfillment he expected it to be. He may think of himself as catering the feast, but in truth, he is the entree. All of us who are weak are guilty of exciting the larceny of the powerful ones who stand ready to take us over, to direct our lives, to trivialize and render meaningless the innocent pursuits of our former days. We could resist them, were it not for the proclivity of our egos to go pride's way and deliver us into their wicked hands.

There exist certain people whose life force comes entirely from the outside, from deception and temptation, and they rule over those they manage to put to sleep.

It is said that a fish stinks from the head down. Whether or not it is true where the fish is concerned, it certainly holds true for the rest of us. A person dies from the head down, and so does a nation. The politicians we elect to rule us are almost invariably female-imprinted vampires, with the power to keep unconscious men asleep in their sins. Why else would we tolerate such leaders? They are the parasites that prey on the life of the people; and the people, not blameless, get the kind of government they deserve.

Creators of illusion can have no power other than the power they gain through deception. They can make us believe (as the result of our emotional response to them) in such a way as to make us reach for all that is wrong. The emotional frustration we suffer as a result feeds them still more power to lead us,

114

and finally kill us. But once you awaken from your hypnotic dream to see by the light of Reality, you destroy their power to deceive and claim you.

The Kingdom of God is already within you and spread over the earth, but men fail to see it; neither can they yet take hold of it firmly enough to manifest its Presence. For that, we need commitment.

We must find salvation from the legacy of original choice, and all we can do to bring it about is yearn to know the purpose for which we were created. From that yearning, the soul will be stressed to wake and lead us with a Right Spirit to freedom from evil's grasp. When you become grounded in the Holy Presence, you will receive His identity; you will be able to do good for the first time in your life.

No mortal has ever sinned out of original choice; none, that is, since Adam, who made that choice. It is our common heritage of compulsion that has led us to harden our hearts and swear our allegiance to evil-doing for the approval of evil people. Be assured. The one who will one day be saved from life's hypnotic spell is the one who questions the sanity and validity of the way he is presently going, and shrinks from the world's acceptance and "love."

The Good Book assures us that "the friendship of the world makes God your enemy."

Everywhere you look, you see those who have been tempted to do wrong defending those who have led them into temptation, and turning on real friends as though they were the enemy. In the same way, our souls have turned against God through the sin of doubt.

7 The Danger of Doubt

Make a person doubt himself—his own common sense, that is—and he immediately becomes suggestible. The door of his psyche flies open, and you can clutter up his consciousness with all manner of nonsense. That monstrosity of so-called art, for instance, sitting outside your local art museum at a cost to the taxpayer of millions of dollars, can have the effect of convincing the self-doubters that just about anything in the world can be called "art." As any successful artist can tell you, if you have enough nerve and you are willing to exert enough hypnotic pressure, you can make *anyone* see *anything* in exactly the way you *want* him to see it. Strangely enough, even when the gullible ones are aware that their leg is being pulled, they will go along with the gag and spend their hard-earned money on the nonsense anyway, as long as you merchandise it in an amusing and clever way. Remember the pet rock craze?

While most church leaders and politicians play this kind of game in order to make big money and create a big following, they are not alone. Our enemies in other countries are playing the same sort of game with us.

They are able to subvert the morals and culture of our own people and either ruin them—period—or simply take them over with their brand of philosophy. It is happening in America right now. Today's leaders can't see this, either because they just won't, or because they are oblivious to the effect they have on people, or because they really know, but are afraid to expose, and thus disarm, their own means of gaining and holding power.

Clearly, we are at a crossroad, and someone must step forward to inform and free the people. Any idea, any notion that is inimical to the best interests of the American people, once planted in the minds of a few gullible (self-doubting) persons, can spread until the sheer weight of mass opinion will carry the more suggestion-proof persons who might not have been paying attention. Bear in mind that doubting what you can see for yourself, the misguided faith in "something out there," disables you from living each moment by the light of your own common sense, thus separating you from reality and opening your mind to hostile, hypnotic invasion.

Do you realize how easy it would be for anyone with some credentials as an artist to command a good price from a museum for a painting that he has "created" by allowing a chicken to wander over a canvas after dipping its feet in some paints? The moment the museum accepts the outrage as a piece of art, every authority-prone weakling is in danger of being sucked in. Of course, there will always be a few viewers with enough faith in their own observation to react adversely, but you can bet your last dollar that there will always be enough self-doubters around to establish the piece of junk as a work of art. Not only that, they will find some reason to admire it even if the fraud is exposed to the public by the artist himself. A sort of cumulative chain reaction sets in and gathers strength until almost everyone has fallen for the new concept, the new way of looking at things. Now, almost anyone can cash in on this mass gullibility to introduce other ideas, ideas that are dangerous, ideas that have the potential to demoralize our entire society. All societies have gone mad in this very fashion, as you can easily see if you care to look back on them, and that fact is the tragedy of culture. Our only defense is a return to reason.

The kind of person who controls you right now is a substitute-elect for the scoundrel in your past who made you doubt yourself, or who upset you into doubting yourself. On a larger scale, it is your king, or president, or dictator.

Perhaps you can look back and throw a spotlight on some distant experience that first shook your faith in yourself. If you can't see clearly that far back, you may be just as well served by taking a good look and becoming aware of who and what are doing it to you now. From the moment you see the ring in your nose, and acknowledge the weakness of faith that allowed it to be put there, you start to be free, your own person, liberated.

In all things, no matter how small or petty the issue seems to be, trust your intuition. Never be swayed by the push of persuasion. You have no need to argue. If you sense something wrong, even if you can't put your finger on it, all you have to do is keep your eyes open and observe. Even when you see that your stand may cost you a valued friendship, your allegiance must be to intuition, not emotion, first, last, and always. The deep knowing that forbids you to believe or to follow without rhyme or reason is infallible. Follow it, and you will never make a wrong choice. If you feel a compulsion to argue, it is nearly always the result of guilt, evoked by a wrong response.

Conflict, anxiety, depression, sickness, disease, and addiction have their roots in an original doubt experience with authority. Doubt always leads to extreme emotional reactions, to a tendency to make up for the guilt of having them by trying to please people. Following people, instead of yourself, you become confused, lost, sick, depressed, hopeless, and perhaps suicidal.

This compulsion to doubt, and to create doubt in others, which almost always originates in the home, is to be found everywhere in the world, especially in so-called educational institutions. Teachers see to it that the children under their care are made to doubt themselves. They seem to look on all those innocent little minds as cluttered canvases that have to be wiped clean by all the forced-learning techniques at their disposal. Only then, can they turn them into masterpieces: robots, with an infallible memory for historical dates; names, places, and other such nonsense.

Intuitive children recognize the dangers inherent in being forced to learn by an intellectual process. At least, they do at first; but once they begin to doubt themselves and give way to the outside pressure, they lose that power of discernment. They find themselves suddenly inundated with knowledge, unable to discern between the good and the bad, forced to learn it all or risk failure. Unable to trust themselves, they grow up uncertain and insecure. And their insecurity often drives them to look for security in all the wrong places: in making money, acquiring fancy possessions, and getting on top of their oppressors. When that fails, they turn to alcohol and drugs.

Of course, the mental confusion, the piling up of disparate facts and accepted notions, in the mind of a person who has lost his unique identity through doubt is made all the worse by his frustration and resentment when he fails to wrest some kind of victory from the hodgepodge of his background and training. He fails, he resents, and his resentment sets him up to fail again.

Some of those who have been made to doubt themselves become so caught up in the process that they throw themselves into more intense study, perhaps of religion, in order to escape the realization of what has been done to them by that very means, hoping somehow to fortify their faith in what they have become. Invariably, they misinterpret guilt and anxiety. Instead of seeing guilt as their "reward" for having copped out on their intuitive knowing, they ascribe the guilt to their failure to "measure up" to the standards set for them by the brainwashers. So, in order to escape the guilt, they tend to set their own standards even higher, thus doing to themselves what their corrupters once did to them.

Once corrupted, people need temptation to reinforce what temptation has done to them. In other words, the lie, once accepted as Truth, becomes the escape from Truth. We are compulsive because of the proclivity of our souls to cling desperately to whatever we have been tricked into believing. And that fact holds true as far as you care to take it—in religion, politics, medicine—from the false heights of "spiritual" cures to the lowest perversions imaginable.

The world has always been controlled by maniacs and psychopaths, and the reason they have so much power is that they know how to appeal to and pressure your ego after it has fallen to their blandishments. They know instinctively how to make you doubt the Truth in yourself.

All ambitious people are either mad or criminally insane. They got that way through having been tempted, or forced, to doubt themselves when they were young. They do become successful, and from a distance, they may not even seem to be mad, but their family and intimate friends know what they are. People say, "Who can argue with success?" Well, in this chapter, I intend to do just that. Some people are successful because other people are weak. So, let's look at how your weakness contributes to the success you can't argue with.

When ambitious people want you to be successful, it is usually for one of the following reasons:

  (1) They want to weaken you in order to use you, to do unto you what was done unto them.

  (2) They feel guilty for their own "success," and as a result, they cannot tolerate your innocence. They will feel more comfortable if you can get into the same boat with them.

  (3) Having failed to be a success, they want to live their lives through you, to be responsible for your success as a means of atoning for the guilt of their own failure. Even in failure, they continue to be driven by the spirit of success and they see themselves as the means of bringing it

to you. The spirit of success is really the spirit of deception.

(4) Some failures *encourage* you to succeed, but secretly they want you to fail; so they will whet your appetite for success in order to feel superior to you when you fail to reach the heights they have envisioned for you.

See how the pressure to succeed can have two opposite effects. It can drive you to "success" or to failure. Either way will serve the purpose of your mad motivator.

You can become upset for either of two reasons: One is by becoming obsessed with ambition, and the other is by being made to doubt yourself. Too much ambition for anything can so unbalance you that you may find yourself being driven instead of doing the driving. An eager beaver is always at a disadvantage, out of control, a helpless slave to monstrous pressure. In hindsight, you might see through the game of power that has been played on you, and, as a loser, you know how upsetting that can be. But quite often you can see through a person's motive *before* you get involved, and you may think, "Are *they* crazy, or am *I* crazy?"

No, you are not crazy for seeing people as they are! Your perception, which can also serve as protection, tends to expose guileful people to themselves, and they feel threatened. By belittling you, however, they might make you think that there is something wrong with you for seeing something wrong with them. And by putting on a super-sweet patronizing attitude, they can often get you to doubt yourself again. Take care not to get caught in the sticky stuff of hypocritical praise.

The moment that vain, ambitious, cruel people make

you doubt what you see in them, you become upset, and then you find yourself powerless to get back on an even keel. As a result, the irrational, rebellious, mean, violent, criminal, confused identity of the worldlings begins to show up in you; and it will seem as though you are the one who is sick and needs help, not they.

It is wrong to be ambitious; that is, to set aside what is right in order to glory in greed. But it is also wrong to let those mean, selfish people cause you to doubt what you see in them. If they are able to do that, they will put out your Light, and you will serve them.

The primary difference between *their* sin (of ambition) and *yours* is that, being closer to Reality, you had the opportunity to guide them—to be the contrast they needed to make them reexamine their motives—and you failed to act on that opportunity. Bear in mind that every person who has been made to doubt himself is *still* a potential child of the Light, a leader, a teacher. If you fail them by keeping silent when others are tempting them to doubt their own common sense, many of those people you might have helped just won't have a chance.

You must learn to trust what is given you to realize in the moment, without becoming upset over what is revealed to you; only then will your mind make you well and whole again. Opening your mind to doubt by the tiniest chink will result in your caving in to doubt forevermore. You will end up in a state of confusion, depression, and rage.

Many of you are probably relieved to see these principles expressed by a survivor, one who confirms what you have suspected all along. But you must do what I have done: You must discover *how* to have faith in what you are given to realize, without becoming resentful and judgmental. Your life depends on turning the tables on those wicked misguided people who are trying to make you doubt yourself, by making *them* doubt *them*selves. Just think of the favor you will be doing them if the correction takes! On top of that, without meaning to do it, you will drive a few stubborn egos up the wall, but you won't be running after them to rub it in, and that's the way it should be.

You have suffered needless mental torture by allowing yourself to become the projection of the cruel sick world around you. And it all began with your doubting, your failure to believe *into* the Truth that was trying to show you what the wicked ones are really like inside.

To a great degree, faith consists of the resistance to the doubt we have been discussing, and as you come back to realizing what faith really is, you will grow in your ability to face cruelty and hypocrisy calmly. You will no longer be tempted to come unglued and make a fool of yourself, but you will be able to use slurs and slaps as just so much manure to promote the growth of the budding new you to its full inner potential.

The sole purpose of temptation is to make you doubt yourself, to make you believe in lies as though they were the truth. Once you give in, you become a slave of the lie-things you come to need to support your corrupted ego against the light of reality.

Ideally speaking, the perfect being has been created by God in His likeness, and he is sustained in that perfection by his continuing devotion and obedience to the divine Presence, which makes itself known to us through the faculty we call "intuition." But once we allow ourselves to become separated from the Ideal Inner Way, through which we might express perfection, the alien identity that has succeeded in separating us from perfection lays claim to our allegiance. Here we have the classic doubt-sin-slave relationship. No one can escape from its legacy of tragedy and death except by reversing his direction—away from original sin, the curse of our heritage, and back to the guidance of Him who created us.

A person at the receiving end of some injustice will either conform by answering in kind, or rebel by concocting a still more sadistic form of retaliation. As the responses escalate, each side becomes more wrong until a knock-down, drag-out war seems to be the only "reasonable" solution. In the case of entire nations, as opposed to individuals, each side adds to the wrong, tempts the other side to still greater acts of violence, and elects a leader to champion the particular neurosis of its own peculiar culture.

You see, then, that evil has always grown to a force of awesome power as the result of our indulging ourselves in some irrational behavior, and then defending it as an inalienable right in the face of challenge. Once a leader has gained power by championing a popular cause, however neurotic its origins, he holds that power by gingering up his following to be more fierce, or more hypocritical; but he will never lead his followers to reason. No demagogue could gain or hold power in a society composed entirely of perceptive and reasonable individuals.

Reasonable children who happen to be born into any of the neurotic factions that exist all over this insane world are a threat, both to the parents and the "culture." Every person in the environment who has anything to do with such a child sees it as his "bounden duty" to destroy him—at least, to render him harmless by getting him to doubt himself enough to turn his back on the testimony of his own senses and God-given intuition. He must be driven mad—at least, changed into a rebel or conformist and forced to accept the label pinned on him, of "ugly duckling," or "rebel without a cause."

A child, before he loses it, does not know that what he has is faith, a guiding Light within himself, outlining Truth. He may assume that it will always be there for him, and he is ill-prepared to realize that he is making a fatal mistake when he starts to listen to those who are determined to put out that Light by making him doubt the reality of its existence within him. So he muddles along to adulthood, taking his direction, first from this one, then that one, and until he realizes that the one true lodestar that could steer him right is the childhood faith he has lost, he will be unable to reverse his direction and get it back.

It could be that you are reading these words because you have arrived at that realization, and you are reaching "out" once more in a desperate search for the key to the way within. If that is so, and you realize that you have been corrupted by the world's way, one of the first things you must do is doubt the "doubts" that have managed to pull you off your center. *If you know you are wrong, you improve your ability to recognize right when it appears.* Just be sure *never* to doubt yourself when you are deeply convinced that you are *right* about what you see, because doubting that *knowing* is what got you into trouble in the first place.

The trouble is that, once you have doubted, the nature of pride grows in you and identifies with the wrong inside the misguided person who made you doubt your own sensibility. Now your conscience becomes your enemy, along with anyone who can see you as you are. *Unconsciously*, you become compelled to make others, in whom the Light shines, doubt the wrong they see in you. So you join the club and set about confusing others with evil little mannerisms of word and deed. The victim of the vampire *becomes* a vampire. Just watch the cruel, mean little things you say to sow confusion in your children and subordinates. Watch, and repent.

I know. You want so desperately to conquer doubt and be filled with real faith again, but I want you to see how you have been going about your search in all the wrong ways.

Let's go over the ground again.

Once you have doubted the Light within you, you take on a world-centered, vain identity; you become wrong and guilty. Once having doubted yourself, you develop a guilt and a fear of being wrong, another fear of becoming wrong again, and yet another fear of being made to doubt yourself again. What you fail to realize is that the doubt engendered by your conscience is a *healthy* form of doubt that can lead you back to repentance and real faith. The Light of Reality may be trying to show you how far you have fallen as the result of your having closed your eyes to it. Unfortunately, your ego rarely interprets the message of the Light in the proper way. Bitter experience has taught you to fear doubt and the guilt it trails in its wake. So your sin-identified self reacts self-righteously against the Light of Reality as though it were the enemy that first introduced you to doubt, and you stubbornly refuse to let it lead you to doubt again. Without realizing what you are doing, you reject its salvation, and you sin again. You become more and more guilty, more and more unsure of yourself.

Sensing your perverted need for faith and confidence, false teachers will rise to the occasion of your need, only too happy and eager to help in all the wrong ways to restore your confidence in your wrong self. No doubt about it; faith is what you need, but not in what doubt has done to you. False faith in your doubt-altered self can lead to manic-depressive psychosis, lifting you to the clouds one moment and dropping you into the dumps the next moment. You must see that anyone who helps you to renewed faith in your fallen self, anything that buoys up your fallen spirit and helps you to fight the good doubt, the saving doubt, is the destroyer in yet another form.

Every person who has ever been made to doubt himself, and has become wrong as a result, will now doubt that there is anything wrong with what he has become. He will be drawn to those who will lend support to his new, doubt-based belief system.

But remember the rule: Doubt can be engendered either by the presence of Truth or the pressure of evil. A true friend can lead you to doubt the way you are going if that way is the wrong way.

When evil is present, either within yourself or in your environment, you can often feel its presence as a force that is tugging at you mentally, offering to save your ego from the nagging little messages of guilt that keep coming to you from your conscience at odd moments. The kind of doubt that will relieve you of that secret anxiety looks like a warm security blanket you can slip into, away from the reality of your failing; in its woolly folds, all will be forgiven and you can rest. Resist that doubt, lest you come to fear Truth and lose yourself in the embrace of evil.

The inherent belief system that enables you to see evil as evil contains the power of peace and calm, an abundant energy field that can draw you away from evil's grasp so that you will move and have your being graciously. But the moment you entertain a grain of doubt as to its rightness and goodness, the force field of faith will collapse and you will fall. Henceforth, you will derive your energy in the animal way, from resentment and anger, and you will forget the human way of faith and obedience. At that moment, you will be taken over by the sin and death personality that flourishes on resentment, and there you will be trapped until you realize the necessity of finding your way back to innocence through repentance.

Repent of doubt. Deeply regret the long-ago weakness that caused you to let go of your belief in yourself. All by itself, that regret will restore to you the "memory" and the courage of those old convictions. Start now; stand up against little offenses. But if you see fit not to, then simply observe error as error. See evil as evil, and wait for the right moment to pounce on it.

In the past, when you failed to observe people with the judgment of discernment, you compensated with the judgment of judgment, with resentment; and resentment always supported the pride that led to still more unworthy feelings and doubts.

You see how incredibly subtle are the machinations of evil. When you are led to doubt yourself, your defenses collapse and in comes pride to compensate you with new defenses, but this time, they are against the Light. What you need now is repentance, not faith in your proud, doubt-altered self.

When you try to make people believe in you, you are actually trying to make them doubt what they already see in you. So if you do manage to make them believe in you, you will have deceived them, done "unto" them what was done "unto" you; for any belief you might find in yourself is false. You can support it only by destroying the Reality relationships of the people around you, because pride can not rule in a vacuum. You will experience shorter and shorter periods of smug self-confidence that will be followed inevitably by more doubt, along with a mad delight in impressing others, or simply destroying them.

You struggle with doubt like one sinking in a swamp. You judge others. You even judge yourself in an attempt to rise higher than the Truth of your own conscience. How can you win? The more you struggle to restore faith—boosting your self-confidence with affirmations and positive thinking—the more you end up lying to yourself, because all your supports are false, unreal. Affirming that the moon is made of green cheese will never make it so. Likewise, a false faith in the false self breaks down in the Light.

The more you convince yourself that you are

wonderful, the more wrong you become, as you try not to see that your growing uncertainty is caused by the very means you are using to shore up your self-confidence. You begin to resent your lack of real faith, and the resentment evolves into fear and a hopeless feeling of being damned forever.

Once again, let's retrace the devolution of doubt:

Doubt leads to the fall, and hence, to sin and guilt. Guilt leads around to doubt again, along with a big helping of resentment, and resentment fuels the pride that drives you to reject the correction of Reality. You end up with so much guilt that you feel hopelessly condemned. So a secret evil inside you confirms a morbid "truth," which compels you to believe in it and resign yourself to it. Even so, you continue to experience what you fear and hate the most—namely, doubt. And whatever you do to get rid of doubt only creates more doubt. Such a doubt-based life leads inevitably to utter despair, a "well-deserved" punishment, and "faith" in the inevitability of death, the domain of the author of all false belief.

The belief in death has, as its basis, a need to have at least one belief beyond the shadow of doubt, but thank God that you retain a capacity for the good doubt, and you are still alive to see through the deceiver.

Surely, you can see the nature of the doubt I am asking you to examine now, and you can see what that good form of doubt is trying to say to you. It is actually the Truth you doubted long ago, asking you to take a good look at what has happened to your life as the result of your ever having doubted the message of His Light. The hopelessness you have felt has never had any real objective reality, so don't throw up your hands and abandon yourself to the hopeless way. The doubt you know now comes from the Light of Reality, making you question the values of the path you are now traveling. True, the way you have been going is hopeless, but *you are not hopeless.*

The separation of your conscious self from your real self, through doubt, leads you to choose one of two completely opposite types of behavior:

(1) You develop into a person who doesn't think much of his own opinions, or of his ability to do and create things. If you happen to do something well and you receive compliments for it, the praise backfires; you can't handle it. So, instead of feeling "built up," you feel unworthy, as though you don't deserve the attention.

Knowing how to handle praise can be a problem for all of us, because anything that feeds the ego a sense of worth is feeding the wrong self and tempting it to grow more wrong. Such a feeling may drive you to excel, or cause you to curl up in a little ball, out of the limelight. You may even seek to make yourself unworthy rather than accept the sense of worth that is productive of guilt. You may have experienced one of these reactions, perhaps even both of them, at different times in your life.

If you have strong feelings of unworthiness, you may take only the humbling kinds of work that support other egos in their efforts to succeed. The types you choose to serve will be "stand-ins" for the kind of people who pulled you off your center in the first place. You don't want to face the dynamics involved in your choice of "service" over "success," so you must keep busy at one meaningless task after another to keep anxiety from catching up with you.

Perhaps you can see that whether you are compensating for guilt by becoming more and more successful, or running *from* success to *escape* guilt and feelings of inferiority, you will wind up with the same prize: more doubt. Any compensation that is aimed at making oneself worthy will always produce the exact opposite effect.

(2) Assume now that you rebel against the idea that you are unworthy, and you set out to prove how very worthy you are. You start to set higher and higher goals and standards in order to spur you on and provide you with a fake hope and a pleasurable distraction from the actual failing they represent. You might also try to prove yourself by disproving or disapproving of others, knocking them down to build yourself up. Or you may tackle difficult projects that challenge you to come up with an ingenious reply.

Where one person tries to escape from the guilt of false self-esteem by making himself small before others, another makes himself big for the same effect. Still another way to build faith in oneself is to enter a profession that is aimed at helping others to believe in themselves. That is the way of the kind of person who becomes a leader, a minister, a businessman, a promoter, an entertainer, a comedian, or a positive thinker. You may unconsciously seek out the kind of leader or mate who will browbeat you in order to make himself feel big if you are the kind of person who wants to feel small. That way, you find your relief where he finds his—for awhile, at least.

Wrong people want to believe in themselves, just like everybody else. Who wants to doubt himself? Weird leaders and weird followers believe that good people are wrong and in need of correction—or destruction, depending on the circumstances. Some of us live in one world, some of us live in another, and the two worlds are at war with each other. Who gets the upper hand over whom will decide the shape of things to come.

Remember what I said earlier: You must be willing to doubt yourself when you are in the wrong, but you must never doubt yourself when you see clearly that you are right and the others are wrong. Your problem is that you have suffered, and become wrong as the result of having doubted God's Light, and now your wrong self is afraid to make the same mistake by doubting again. But if you will just face the facts by the light of your new understanding, you will find that the way out of your dilemma is simple. First, realize that you have erred; don't doubt that the first doubt, the one that bonded you to the outside world, was a mistake, because it surely was. The trouble is that you have taken on the nature of that mistake so completely that you think you are defending your *self* when you defend *it*. By defending the evil that has made a home in you, you are defending the wrong against the Light.

Do you see a difference between the healthy and an unhealthy way of doubting? God has supplied us with the intuition to make us doubt the rightness of all that is wrong, and that is good, but you must be able to discern the difference between the intuitive doubt and the worldly doubt that seeks to pull you into the worldly

135

system. If you fail in this, you will develop such a fear of doubting that you will come to fear Truth itself, and you will close the door on your own salvation.

Doubt was, and still is, the original sin. Doubting Truth is part of the legacy that has come down to us. It shows up in our tendency to believe more in what people say than in what our own common sense tells us. We do not understand that the Light (now refracted by our doubt into something we feel as painful anxiety or conscience), which can reveal all things to us plainly, without words, radiates from God, the very God that Adam doubted, thanks to the serpent. Through Adam's belief in the serpent, we have become progeny of the serpent, and the doubt of Truth still holds sway over our minds and hearts. And it will continue to do so until the day we discover Truth for ourselves. We learn, if we are capable of learning, that all our tragedy, suffering, even our dying, have grown from the seed of doubt. To doubt good is to believe evil. But conversely, to doubt evil is to restore our belief in the good.

Your believing soul creates an environment around itself through which it can express. As you will see, when you reverse the process of doubt and take hold of the courage of your convictions, beautiful things will begin to occur all around you. You will feel richly blessed, a feeling that you have never been able to experience before, because you were living from a misguided faith.

"Have faith!" preach the preachers. "Believe in yourself!" shout the positive thinkers. But try as you will to believe in yourself, you end up with a greater doubt. You made a big mess of your life because you believed those who encouraged you to believe in what was false about yourself, which is precisely what made those tempters so believable. Since the confidence they have "sold" you is in the wrong self, you wind up in a state of conflict with your true Self, the one that has not completely lost touch with the presence of Reality and is trying to call you back.

Surely you must see the joy that comes to those who realize the truth of Truth. Your faith in other people and in your doubt-altered self has made you an enemy of God. And all the time, you thought you were on His side!

Belief joins you to good or to evil. Believe in this person or that, and you find that you are involved with this person or that, the evolved extension of what is inside them.

It follows, then, that true belief can also join you to God. You already have the power that can believe *into* God and restore you to His Presence. You have only to realize the folly of ever having doubted Him. Realize now the folly of believing in those misguided people who have helped you to believe in yourself, the self they have made over in their image.

Believe! Stand firm in the secret observation post of your God-given intuition. From there, you can truly see where people are coming from. Never doubt the Light that outlines subtle shades of meaning and motive in a wordless way. See how your belief joins you to the Truth that sets you free.

8 The Way Back

If you are a searching person, you realize that all your problems and conflicts have been caused by the way you have been responding to the pressures and stresses of everyday life. The stress bond you have developed with many pressure sources is hypnotic, and the control it exerts over you is similar to the control you should have over you own mind and emotions—from within.

In the instant that you allow the rapport with your higher consciousness to be ruptured, you open the door to the outside pressure source, and you bond with it. You become externalized. After that, everything you do is motivated by your desire to conform or to rebel, because you have lost the ability to see calmly and objectively.

As the pressure source acts out its will through us, we will think we are acting for ourselves; but because we have dramatized the will of others, we have become imprinted with *their* identity and lost our own. The identification is obvious to others and even to ourselves, if we care to look, in the case of rebel identification. After all, conformists don't make waves. But no matter what you do, you gather your identity, nature, and purpose from the sensuous world like any of the lower animals, and thus you create conflict with the Real Self, the human Self that is waiting to unfold from within. No one can find rest until he finds his way back to his own center of dignity, autonomous motivation, Grace.

There lives within you an omniscient Inner Presence who can have His way through you; but to experience the God Presence, you must come up through the layers of your unconscious thinking to the *sanctum sanctorum,* the Inner Presence. To do so, you must learn to be still, and to suffer in patience the redeeming pain of the Inner Pressure, and to capitulate to Him in much the way you are now yielding to external, evil pressures.

We can trace our individual form of suffering back to the particular pressures and conditioning of our early lives; for once we establish a pattern of response to a particular source of irritation, our egos will continue to be attracted to those persons who best represent it. It's not by accident that men get their mothers back in their wives. They just can't see an oddball as marriage material—unless, of course, their mother was that very kind of oddball.

Your troubles cling to you for two basic reasons: partly because of the conditioned need itself, and partly because of the complicated pattern created by your repeated animal responses to everything that evokes it, and thus blocks the real you from coming through.

The conflict between the real you and the you that has evolved from conditioned responses will eventually drive you to seek escape; but your efforts along that line only add to a growing list of irritations and sources of excitement, leading to more conditioned responses.

You may be tired of living like a yo-yo—up in the clouds one minute, down in the dumps the next. It's depressing, and you may feel trapped, because your emotional reactions to pleasure and pain have worn down your level of awareness to the point that you see no way out.

But the solution is really very simple. You must come back to the aware state of consciousness that you lost back there in your childhood through your conditioning to various pressures and pleasures. Let go of the hardness of heart, the resentment turned back on yourself, that has become a barrier against the clear perception of your faults.

The way you react determines the way you develop mentally and physically. It is the key to the quality of life you will know. You are inspired by what motivates you; so you become outwardly like what you respond to in secret, be it good or evil.

The way you grow has a lot to do with your perception, what you observe about life and about yourself. What you observe about yourself after you have reacted to pressure can be a valuable learning experience; that is, if you do not immediately dismiss your reaction with some flimsy excuse—like, "he sure had it coming"—but continue to observe your upset state long enough to know that you are trying to find comfort and justification in a lie. You had your chance to respond calmly, with true understanding, and you blew it by reacting on an animal level. Of course, there are those to whom emotional intrigue and confusion are the very elixir of life, and they will become ever more adept at the Devil's alchemy, as they turn shame into self-righteousness. Whether we are lie-led or Truth-led will always depend on the inclination of our soul.

The ability to come up with the correct response for each moment develops with your steadfast perception of the unseen source and purpose of all your secret impulses. If your source is Good, in that your will is to do His will, you will one day discover your true Self. If, on the other hand, your source is evil, you will know the horror of that.

Your attitude will determine the way you respond. If you are vain and greedy, you will be blinded to Reality by the exciting prospect of easy personal gain; you will reach for the carrot dangling on the stick of temptation that cultivates and calls to your donkey desires. Evil will set your goals and determine your motivation and control your life. As you struggle to fulfill "your" ambition with resentment and frustration, growing always in the wrong way, you degenerate amid your escapes and fantasies.

According to the inclination of your soul, a will—not yours—lives in you. You grow to realize and serve the source of your motivation, whether you like it or not.

Nothing can be any better than its source. You reflect what energizes you. You dramatize where you are coming from in everything you say and in the way you behave. Everything you do or say manifests the immaterial, unseen source of your motivation. If you are growing from a proper source, you are honestly honest, in concert with your real Self. Otherwise, you are animated by Hell, a slave of the devil, a liar, full of deceit and excuses, bound to do harm. You will experience conflict, fear, and an insecurity beyond cure, until you realize and repent of the error of your way.

The excitement of emotion, especially resentment, expresses itself in a body language that reveals the nature of a person's failing and the extent of his obedience to the spirit of his master evil. A fine writer has said, "No Man is an Island." I'd like to add: neither is he invisible to those who have eyes to see and ears to hear the language of his body. Yet, I would not deliberately lure you to the service of Good by causing you to fear your high visibility, lest you set about hypocritically to cover your shame by doing and saying all the right things for all the wrong reasons. The shame that redeems is not the shame we feel at being discovered by our peers. It is the shame we feel in the Presence of our Creator for having disobeyed Him, the shame that causes us to abandon Pride's way, and return to the service of Good, let the chips fall where they may.

Encoded in your body cells is the memory of an ancient and tragic story of pride, encompassing all the times you have stepped outside the boundary of reason. To this very day, you are still doubting yourself, your real Self, that is, and selling out for some imagined ego advantage. Fear, frustration, and violent emotions bear witness to your allegiance to that far-off, yet ever-present, primeval cause.

A searching person seeks that special state of consciousness that allows him to believe, and so respond to, what is right deep in his heart; he seeks freedom from the violence of external conditioning, from the compulsion to sin. A vain person, not able to face the reality of his slavishness, continues to lose awareness and to get his high by responding, growing, and being promoted by, the wrong source.

Even your health depends on what energizes you. If you are excited, upset, and turned on by all the wrong things, you can be drained of energy. At the other extreme, you could work up so much nervous energy that you could burn out before your time. Some of us are so responsive to our environment that we respond and give up energy. Others of us revel in feeding off of those energies. Believe it or not, our life-support systems can be literally converted to service the terrible life demands of the successful egos around us. I have dealt with this phenomenon more fully in another book: *How to Conquer Suffering Without Doctors.*

Very ambitious, highly-motivated persons obtain extra drive at the expense of those around them. They do it either by needling their victims, or by exciting them with illusions of grandeur and vain promises of gain. Pretending love for you, they can disturb you into giving up a life force, which they feed on like the psychic vampires they are. Such is the nature of their "success" and your failure. Most of us have felt drained, disillusioned, and depressed by people like this. Now you know the reason why.

"Libido" is a word used by psychologists to describe a primitive psycho-emotional vitality that the vain ego derives from aroused, primitive, biological urges that direct him toward the realization of his dreams, sexual love being its grossest manifestation. As your ego strives to realize its implanted ambitions, it loses its balance and falls to a level where it needs such emotional drives to keep going. In the process, your entire nature undergoes a *physical* change that leads eventually to death.

144

And because your ego continues to draw on those lower animal vitalities, rather than on the higher instincts, your body experiences many devolutionary adaptive changes. On the psychological level, you cultivate more excuses and fantasies to enable your ego to elude the truth of what it is becoming. So, each time you fall asleep to Reality, you "awaken" on a lower level of animal existence.

You may develop cancer as the result of draining body cells of their vital force, causing them to rebel against the tyranny of a never-satisfied, life-hungry ego. Impatience, frustration, and resentment are the energy sources of a proud and fallen ego, devoid of gracious power. For example, if the hatred of poverty drives you to become rich, you have only to think of how it was to be poor to get the energy you need for motivation.

Once you have responded to the subtle presence of temptation, your nature begins to exist around the source of its change. What you once hated, and secretly always will, you also need, and you may think of that need as "love." To put it another way, the corrupted self develops a need to be turned on by the very evil that turned it "off" to Reality. Thus, the real self becomes the helpless prisoner of the life-hungry needs of the false self. So you may become drained by the ego demands of the monstrous egos of others, or it may be your own false self that is doing the draining. Either way, this energy-draining process accounts for over 100,000 diseases, with cancer the number 1 killer.

A person can grow to be a beautiful human being, or a sickly, degenerate, gross animal, deceiving and being deceived, draining, or being drained of, life. Your secret motive will determine the energy source you choose to draw from. If you are vain and self-serving, the libido, love/hate energy, drained from self, things, or other people, will be the only energy available to you. You will need it to attain to the forbidden, or perhaps to maintain a self-righteous external facade.

The need to escape, the lust for reassurance and love, the need for power and self-importance, force your ego to dig into your mental gut for primitive animal drives to replace the true life you forfeited in order to be proud. All ambitions, goals, and self-righteous roles demand excitement from the lower-animal self in order to block the passage of Real life, patience, love, and Grace.

You would always be perfectly safe, in complete control of your own life, if you were to remain within the protective boundaries of your reason. But having been tricked, tempted, and aggravated away from its center, your ego has lost its way and doesn't know how to come home again. Wandering around in a thinking and feeling world, you become more and more confused, more subject to deception, simply because you have lost the way to see clearly.

Your present sensitivity to pressure continues to grow in direct proportion to the degree of your being lost in your thoughts as the result of having doubted yourself. Remember, every emotional upset or fear can be traced back to some obvious or subtle form of egocentricity. But if you will see the lie for what it is, in the light, you can doubt the lie. And doubting the lie will free you to believe the Truth again.

With your ego centered, expressing native wisdom

and goodness, you would be less subject to the dehumanizing pressures of evil. So if you are upset, overreactive, nervous, fearful, and guilty, take it as a sign that you have lost your way. Somewhere down the line, you have responded to, and are following, evil. Your resentment and impatience bear witness to your wrong allegiance.

Surely you have observed the vicious cycle yourself. Something upsets you, and it changes the way you think and feel. You feel doomed, damned, and depressed. You can't control your thoughts, and your health suffers. You develop headaches and other assorted aches and pains. You take it out on your family until they are more miserable than you are. You try to forget what is happening to you, but you can't. You either can't sleep, or you sleep too much, as the result of exhaustion and the need to escape.

If only you could find the power to keep pressure from getting under your skin by remaining calm *at the point of stress,* you could render yourself impervious to assault, psychic or physical. You could not possibly fall prey to morbid states of mind and project them to your loved ones.

Emotion is the key to your conditioning, and as they say, "Nothing succeeds like success." If you couldn't control yourself the first time, you will have even less control the second, third, and fourth times. Simply by responding, becoming upset, you deliver the control over your thoughts and feelings into the hands of others. Henceforth they control your moods, and they can manipulate you into rebelling or conforming, whichever suits their purpose. Suppose someone tells you that you are no good, and you react so violently to the suggestion that it finally becomes a fact. Or you struggle to compensate and free yourself of the suggestion by "showing them." Either way, you will have used up your energy playing *their* game, proving *them* right or wrong, instead of discovering your own unique purpose on earth.

Pressure and stress are synonyms for the motivation that springs from an evil source. If a person can upset you, he can motivate you, and that fact is the key to all your conflicts. If you react in a wrong way, you grow in a wrong way. If you react in a right way (by not reacting with emotion at all), you grow from within and unfold like a flower drinking in the sun.

A person grows, not by learning, but by impulse. When you respond in a right way, the source of that response not only governs the way you grow; it reveals itself both to you and to others. The after-the-fact observation of your growing leads to true understanding, and this understanding strengthens your belief in what is true, leading to your greater obedience to principle and an unshakable confidence in your own true self.

Sooner or later, your secret life will manifest itself openly. If something evil has been leading you astray, your reactions will have imprinted you with its nature. Your worldly understanding of yourself and of life in general will be composed of excuses to rationalize wickedness. By your responses you reveal your source of motivation. Obey the wrong impulse to your peril.

Do you want to free yourself from evil's grasp? Then, you must examine your emotional responses; become aware of what entices, upsets, or excites you.

Watch the emotion that rises when you want something too much. Watch the slow boil of anger, pride, and judgment.

As your soul yearns for the truth, Reality will begin to lead you through a series of wordless revelations. Never consult your intellect, lest you be prompted by the devil that lurks down there. Approach each problem with the awareness of Now. Wait until the time is right for action without submitting the decision to some elaborate reasoning process. Be patient. True life does not filter down through the intellectual processes for you to consult. Faith is a "mindless" trust in God, the source of the faith impulse; for what is seen is made by what does not appear.

The longing for the ground of one's being is called love, and its fulfillment is happiness, a heaven on earth. But, even as goodly souls yearn to bond with the source of their being, the corrupt souls also long for what it is that made them evil, and the result is chaos.

True longing, then, draws true fulfillment. The result of acting out an intuitive impulse is a discovery experience called understanding, a greater appreciation of the invisible God who draws you close.

Intellectualized knowledge, even Scriptures, should never govern our lives. *Truth must ever govern the ways of a soul yearning for truth.* The mysterious longing (love) and true behavior that is pleasing to God brings an infilling approval to spiritual or emotional need, even as the longing of prideful persons draws to them the lowly approvals and satisfactions that animate the brutish self.

Pride is the culprit, the major cause of all problems,

fears, and guilts; and pride always draws to itself an invisible impulse from its evil source.

Emotionality is evidence of the underlying wrong of pride, the energy needed by an ego that is separate from God. Something wicked inside a fallen being wants him to be impatient, and it is always drawing him to the wrong people and to activities that lead inevitably to frustration.

People seduce you by appealing to your lowly needs with appropriate offerings of excitement or comfort. Soon, all your reactions become compulsive, and your mind swirls with excuses. You *cannot* stop being afraid and guilty because you cannot stop responding to demands, pressures, and suggestions. As you grow spiritually toward the source of evil and disaster, you are drawn to tragedy like a moth is drawn to a candle.

Using the energy of resentment, your ego struggles to save itself, but the sheer vanity of such a struggle, implemented as it is with ideas, feelings, and reliance on other people, pulls you in deeper and causes you still more guilt. It is one thing to become involved with wrong, but to try to save yourself with false virtue and innocence, and not face up to having made the mistake, creates an even greater wrong.

As a creature of relativity, separated from the ground of your true being, you can no longer be subject to the inner world of conscience, because you have become subject to what has yanked you away from its gravitational pull.

When you reach toward glorious goals, you leave behind your humanity. Then, you tend to reject the truth concerning what has happened to you. You complicate matters still further with your escapes, distractions, and comforts that look like solutions. Guilt and resentment compel you to rebel against the true knowledge, and you sin again and again by wrestling with the problem instead of seeking to know the cause.

Next to the lack of faith, ego-emotional materialism presents your biggest hazard on the way back to reality. The things you use for distraction and a feeling of security become an environmental refuge. Whenever you stand to lose material things that you "had to have" to gratify your ego, or even worse, when you can't even acquire them, "king" ego feels hopeless, terrified, shaken with insecurity. If the security you seek happens to take the form of a person, or lover, you might feel the special kind of resentment called jealousy; and because jealousy aggravates libido, you feel diminished beyond endurance. Through resentment, you become less of a person, and you feel self-conscious, inferior, and guilty.

There is nothing wrong with working to acquire material objects—some of them, after all, are necessary for survival—but they should never be used primarily to feed your hungry ego. Or to get in the way of your seeking the purpose for which you were created, which is certainly more important than *looking* important. As long as you put first things first, you will know naturally what is important for you to have, and you will meet each new situation with a proper response. That is, you will not respond at all to pressure, but you will develop from your inner wisdom.

When you "die" to the call of sin, you lose all fear and anxiety. You also lose the desire for drugs, drink, cigarettes, or any other kind of comfort or escape. Always remember that "cures" and escapes are really different forms of temptation, so that whatever tempts you to become wrong and comforts you in that wrong is responsible for your fall.

If you are fully committed to what is right, you will be responsible and loyal in your relationships with others. You will have the staying power to see things through.

The power to stand firm and unresponsive to pressure must always be preceded by your commitment to what is right in your heart. It is that commitment that enables you to grow, in spite of all the pressures and temptations of the world around you. If you find yourself becoming more "your own person," less responsive to stress of all kinds, you will actually see the extent of your commitment to what is right in your heart.

Every foolish person has a date with tragedy. Every wrong response sets him up to respond even more emotionally and violently the next time. Then, one day, when he needs wisdom and composure to save the day, he will know only fear and rage.

9 Be Still and Know

Awareness is a favorite subject of mine for reasons I hope will soon be clear to you. True awareness, you see, is the very key to life. Your own awareness may be increasing or diminishing, and, as I have already pointed out, you may actually think that your awareness is increasing when it is actually diminishing, thanks to your involvement with the unreal, make-believe world of imagination.

Losing yourself in ideas and images is your ego's way of idealizing itself. You become preoccupied with image building, a form of self-deception that enables you to forget your real-life failures. Your embarrassment over the clumsy way you handled a business deal might be too much for you to face; so you take off on a Walter Mitty fantasy, in which you become a great tycoon with the power to make or break the poor fool who just got the better of you in real life. As you continue to indulge yourself in these flights of fancy, you develop the creeping delusion that your consciousness is actually expanding, that you are more abundantly alive, on top of things.

The truth of the matter is that this delusion can lead

only to depression, conflict, fear, and guilt. Once you set out on the mind-game journey away from the Light, shame follows, forcing you to burrow deeper into the dark, illusory world of intellectual escape. Beneath the superficial mental fantasy there lurks a nightmarish world of reality that flashes intermittently across the downward path, causing you to flee faster from the light, like a spiritual gopher running for its life, trying to get away, even from the truth of what it is doing.

The ego principle of pride is this: As long as you are not aware of what is wrong, you simply have to think you are right; and once you establish a fixation to thought as the means of dealing with Reality, you will go to absurd extremes.

Just how aware are you this minute? Become conscious of what I am trying to convey to you, without trying to remember the exact words. Become conscious of yourself, of the here and now, as these words pass by the grandstand for your observation. Awareness of here and now is an eternal quality. If you could become progressively more aware, you would become alive in an eternal way.

Dying is the movement away from awareness, and death is the ultimate loss of the consciousness of life. A blow to the head could cause you to lose consciousness, and enough of them over a period of time would result in death.

Death, to reverse the biblical word order, is truly the wages of sin. And the original sin was man's separation from God to be a god. For most of us descendants of the first sinner, we have moved so far from that original Oneness with our Creator that sin, for us, usually assumes the form of an escape from the awareness of how wrong we are, and how much more wrong we are becoming in our ego descent. But if you could always be aware in a special way, you might never see death at all. If you find the secret way to reverse (not increase) your awareness from its state of falling, you might live forever.

A consciousness of Reality, then, becomes consciousness that is in control of itself, its life, and its environment. Eternal life, however, can only be found in the final at-one-ment (atonement) with God.

The first step toward the secret of eternal existence lies in the soul's yearning for the Eternal One who created man and woman in the beginning. The Creator of life is also the creator of our consciousness of life, and His Presence is the reason for our self-consciousness. He is the Great Awareness from Whom awareness originates. From His Presence springs the only kind of knowledge that can completely change a man from the inside, through repentance and humility.

Look: The eye sees by the light of the sun. What use is the eye without a sun? Deprived of light, surely the eye would cease to exist! So it is with God, our Parent Consciousness. When we shut our mind's eye to His illumination, we wither away. The Light within is not only able to metamorphose as a body, through the inner eye, but it can also shine through the mind's eye of the soul and give direction to that body.

Alas for the proud one who follows the opposite course, who runs away from whatever makes the soul conscious of God, so that, in his pride, he can become god himself, the only consciousness in the universe.

Alone, lost in his creation, he tries to find himself through everything he experiences. He uses knowledge to effect his escape from God to be God.

Remember that Adam sinned by *knowing* God and evil. The word "know" is often used in the Bible to mean "to be intimate with." As in, "Adam *knew* Eve, and she conceived." Do you see how that applies to your own life? Does not your own desire to play God cause you to get involved with the information in your imagination? Does not imagination seduce your soul? Does not knowledge tempt you to "know" yourself as God when you give knowledge the top priority in your consciousness?

Most of us are guilty of playing God, but we rarely realize what we are doing, simply because our shutting down of the perception of God renders us unable to realize anything as it exists in reality. We may acquire knowledge, but we cannot understand what we know. We think that if we know something intellectually, we understand it. That simply is not true. Our awareness gradually diminishes to such a degree that we cannot be aware of its happening; we are too busy compensating for its loss with the delusion of growth we derive from our imagination. We also fail to see where our many unconscious animal drives and goals are coming from, simply because we are so involved with our unconscious memories that we understand only the things we want to understand. True understanding would be too painful for a proud ego to bear. All that a stupid soul wants to do is to be conscious of himself as *the* Reality, through his emotionally-sustained imagination.

Although they might be educated, few men ever

understand anything at all about the meaning of existence. Understanding is a special kind of intimacy with God that can be realized *only* if you can divorce yourself from the world of your imagination. Realization, as opposed to rote knowledge, comes from the light filtering down through your rising consciousness. Understanding is *in*-formation, a growing by knowing God, rather than a growing out of environmental pressure. In our pride, we have become formed by, and subject to, environment, abode of the spirit of deception that works its evil through knowledge.

Bear in mind that either we know the Truth, or we know ourselves "as" the Truth. There are really only two states of consciousness—the self-righteous, but less conscious state of consciousness—that of knowing oneself as the Truth—is one of total involvement with worry, thought, dream stuff, fantasy, and the sustaining environment.

Remembering, then, is really a way of forgetting Reality, a way of becoming God. By remembering who you are, you fail to realize the lows to which you have sunk. By seeking knowledge and getting lost in its storehouse, the imagination, we lose true understanding as we revel in the false concepts of our culture.

Apparently, man is the only animal capable of making himself sick by trying to be something that exists only in his imagination. He alone experiences the consequences of thinking he is something he is not.

Everything you do is aimed at making you the creator of a little counter-universe, in which you are the lone and lonely conscious center. But aloneness can be a terrifying thing inasmuch as a lone self, a self apart from Truth, is also a dying self. Therefore, along with aloneness you feel the fear of dying.

The stubborn, dying soul likes to wallow in an illusion of existence, but sooner or later, it must be forced to realize the price it is paying for its sin. And as it flips between realizing the horror of dying and escaping from that realization into its fantasies, it continues to die.

But all is not lost. When you allow yourself to see by a greater Truth than yourself, you start to grow in the Light like a tree. A sapling absorbs energy from the sun through its leaves, and as it develops, many more leaves appear, in order to catch still more sunlight through the process of photosynthesis, and thus assure the growth of the main body of the tree. The leaves take life from the sun and "realize" that light into a tangible earthly form, an expression of the sun's presence in the material world.

So we have the sun and the expression of the sun, coming through the plant's soul: the leaf. Do you see how the leaf resembles the soul of man? Leaves metamorphose the plan of light into the bodies of larger plants; and that is exactly the relationship you should have with the Light within you, the Creator of the sun and all that is. But you, as an individual ideation of God, cannot realize God and play God at the same time, any more than the flower can be a sun and still remain a flower. So if you are sick and dying, it is because you are proud, trying to play God in some unrecognized way.

Like the tree, you should content yourself with being the expression of the Light, and thereby a witness to the Light, growing in the Light to become a mature

158

child of the Light. And this marvelous "psychosynthesis" requires a special attitude of consciousness, which, at a certain level of ascent, transmits and transmutes greater amounts of spiritual Light: first, to metamorphose as a body with its particular character, and then to extend itself into deeds that project a world of paradise into being. Only a consciousness that seeks the Light, and doesn't stand in the Light to *be* the Light, can bring Heaven's plan down to earth.

To acknowledge the Light, then, is to live in awe and wonder; and to stand in awe, in open-mouthed wonder, is to worship. Just as the flower's receptivity to the sun is also the flower's love for the sun, so is our need for God's love for Him. Likewise, the life in the leaf, the soul that yearns for the Light that created it, feels affection even for its need for God's Own Self to exist in it. It comes to pass that the source, and the expression of the source, are as one; yet, they are also separate. Like a leaf plucked from its source of light and life, we also cease to exist away from our Light.

To be receptive to God's light is to be like a plant growing toward the sun, compatible and affectionate, with the soul leaves reaching for, and being enveloped by, the sun. A tree growing toward the light will use all of its stored energy to work its way through the undergrowth toward its source of light and life.

Now, how much different are you, O ye of little faith? Are you not potential children of the Light? Or will you be content to be children of the darkness, mushrooms feeding off one another's decadence? Believe it or not, there are those whose consciousness has descended to such a lowly level of existence. And

159

so, as you die to those who keep you from the Light, your consciousness seeks its own prey to live from emotionally. (I have treated this at greater length in *How to Conquer Suffering Without Doctors.*)

The consciousness you require for your spiritual growth is not far from the consciousness that gives you the ability to understand me, as it is speaking through me into your dark world of worry and fear, talking to you in your sleep, calling to you down there in the depths of the jungle of your fantasy, in the depths of your confusion and despair.

Why are you down there? Why is it that you have descended so low? Is it not because pride called you down to receive the knowledge of glory? Or is it the pride of others, who do not wish you to understand, that stands in your way?

You have been brought down by being pridefully caught up in the pursuit of things that glorify, things that give you a lift, a sense of consciousness, an image, a sense of awareness of beauty, a sense of goodness, of being some kind of paragon. Immersed in pride, your ego experiences a delusion of grandeur and it escapes into sensual reverie and nostalgic memories. You are living with what you want to believe about yourself and what you think you want out of life. Memories entertain, delight, and tantalize your stupid soul. And you are, without realizing it, whoring with Hell itself.

You are divorced from Reality because Hell has seduced you into a dream state and taken over Reality's role in your fallen consciousness. Now, the condemnation and pain you feel is for your identification with the spirit of pride. You feel the pain of its hell, and you are dying of guilt, hopelessness, and despair, simply because your descent into unconsciousness is guided by the master deceiver who has taken you over.

There is, after all, another conscious intelligence in the universe, other than yourself and the God reality you are yet to realize. It is the south pole of the universe in which God represents the north pole, and everything within that universe has a polarity, a leaning one way or the other. Just as the nature and spirit of God comes to you through your love of Truth, so does the spirit of the lowly reality live through you by way of your love of deception.

There are two leading, educating spirits to need and embrace—good and evil—and you are caught somewhere in between. Depending on the proclivity of your consciousness, you will be drawn one way or the other.

Once you begin the downward journey, you will think you are moving up, but the "high" you feel is the soul's delight in its illusions of grandeur, because the pain of conscience disappears the moment you step away from truth into the "saving" fantasy of mental delight. Of course, the morning after the night before, when the smoke of excitement and pleasure has cleared, you will face once again the Light of Reality. You see, the True Reality, the reality you are running from, tends to outline the cruel reality of which you have become the projection.

You cannot *be* God, but you can respond either to Him or to the devil; so you are either a servant of heaven or a slave of hell. You are self-conscious (humble) before heaven, or inferior toward hell, and the more you struggle against that truth, the more inferior you become. Your unwillingness to face the first Truth intensifies your fear of facing the second truth.

The hellfire-and-damnation preachers be damned! I am not speaking to you on that level to frighten you. I am speaking to you, from a real and present perspective on life, about what is wrong with your life here and now, and about what is, and what is not, a figment of your imagination. Beyond the realm of imagination, on the otherworldly side of your senses, you find the demon spirit of the imagination, the old snake in the grass, the serpent of old, who, through the appeal to pride, cast himself first into Eve and then into Adam. He is the court jester of your kingly soul, your seducer, quietly suggesting your way to "glory," leading you to a dying that appears to be a living, through a diminishing consciousness that thinks it is expanding.

Men were never created to live in tragedy, disease, poverty, and sickness. Or under insane political and religious systems, or to live like vegetables, or like madmen under the tyranny of death. They were created for a very special purpose, a very special plan your eye has not yet seen or ear heard, because it is yet to enter into your heart. But that plan can unfold in you, and it will, if that is what you want more than anything else. Simply listen to the echo in your soul that testifies to what I am saying to you and see where you stand now. Realize that every error you have made has been caused by your ego's state of mind. You have become involved with the evil shepherd because the insincere yearning of your soul attracted him to you—and you to him.

Unconsciously, your fallen nature has adapted to a

sensuous world, the projection of hell on earth. As a result, you feel compulsive, guilty, anxious, self-conscious, and afraid. But perhaps your greatest fear is of discovering the inferiority and fallibility that lead to death. You started out to discover your infallibility and superiority; you wanted the world to look up to you as the Light of Heaven. You thought that once you found your glory you would never know death. Thoughts of death rarely entered your consciousness while you were busy building your world. You were so busy proving something to yourself that the effort became a kind of eternal dedication, a labor of love. Because Truth does not exist for you at such times, you feel your consciousness soaring higher and higher, oblivious to the passage of time, until you finally hit bottom and become aware of your old nemesis, the negative truth about your negative self.

Whether you finally feel the nudge of the True Reality and back off, or you come to a screaming halt at the gates of Hell, you will see one reality by the Light of the other. You will come to fear death as well as life, and fear will turn to panic at the sight of your hopeless inferiority. Realize before it is too late, then, that this panic is the selfsame reaction that started you on your compulsive journey toward Hell when you first sought refuge from Reality.

Panic is a fear of the truth; it symbolizes your rejection of Reality. And no matter which way you go, or how hard you run, you must eventually accept *some* reality, whether you like it or not. If you are hellbound, you will automatically accept hell. You will always be drawn toward the lesser, the evil, reality as the result of your rejection of the True Reality. You reject Reality because you are proud and stubborn in your way, so when you refuse to face the second horrible truth by the light you left behind, it means that you just don't want to realize the truth of what you are and where you are headed. There is still no place in your heart for repentance. It also means that you cannot bear to realize there is something greater than you, even if it's the devil himself.

The day you start to play god and to make judgments and plan goals, rather than allow yourself to realize life's purpose, is the day you begin to die the second death. It was just such an aspiration that caused Adam to die as a conscious being, and come alive as a self-conscious inferior brute. The serpent that felled him is still around to help his progeny build their egos and thus finish the job he started through what we refer to affectionately as "progress." Everything we do, we do to glorify, or quietly cure, our inferiorities without having to recognize the original and fatal flaw in our nature.

The entire world is running from the Truth. Suffering, disease, tragedy, famine, and war are closing in from every side. Even when we have everything we want or need, we are depressed and in despair for our lives, wasting away to nothingness. Again and again, we fall prey to the same old evil in one of its many disguises.

What are you trying to find through your various experiences? Are you not trying to discover that you are God? Are you not looking for that ultimate experience that will help you to recapture the memory of who you are? Are you not vaguely seeking the lost power of your own mind, while closing your eyes to the way your soul rejected it?

It has been said that the universe is the mind of God; so, like God, we seek our own special world amid the knowledge gleanings of our minds, but the only world we can find there is a world of Hell's creation.

Beware of the snake in the grass, the serpent of old, who cast itself into Eve, and through Eve, into man, and who now is incarnated in the worldly people who speak the serpent's words in praise of the "good" (sensuous) life—the glory of power, of riches, of accomplishments, of the greatness of man, of his glorious evolution. Beware of the appeal to your ego in any form: religious, political, medical. Beware of a cure that does not point to the causative factor, the personal failing that makes a cure necessary. Any other cure is another disease in disguise. Watch out for the devil who might speak as I do of expanding consciousness. Test him against your inner Light, for if you are sincere about finding God, you will be able to distinguish between us and to know whether we are both coming from the same place.

I warn you to be alert in all your encounters with people. You may be playing with fire. Whether you grow toward the Light or toward death will depend on the way you meet the subtle temptations of life. Do you detect deception and meet it with wisdom and grace, or are you easily pulled in?

A consciousness that is eternal is a consciousness that never dies, nor does the body in which it dwells. Eternal life is the purpose for which man was created; but in order to know that life, the soul must be proved true—it must not be afraid to give up the kind of life it has inherited.

Goodness cannot be physically created, and born of an egg or a seed, like a bird or a bee or a flower or a tree. All natural life is compulsively obedient to natural law and is therefore incapable of love.

The atoms of the universe are not free to obey or to disobey the law. The laws they obey are immutable. Were they free to disregard their orbits, the universe could not exist as we know it. The universe exists as it does because of an orderly arrangement, under laws that bind every living and non-living thing to its proper orbit and cycle. Man alone has been given a choice between good and evil, to love God or to know himself as God by living in his brains, instead of remaining conscious and objective in the Light.

The vain person wishes no consciousness of Truth, so he denies God and creates his own god by living in his own mind. Of course, once he has convinced himself of his godhood, he just can't be wrong, can he? The games we play with our minds can fill volumes. Have you recognized some of your own?

The Scripture tells us that we inherit the sin of pride, that we are not free moral agents. What does this mean? Not free? Slaves of sin?

As soon as we reach the threshold of awareness, we feel anxiety from an unknown source, and we shrink from knowing what it is. It feels as though we are afraid to know something about ourselves. At that point, we escape into sensuality, friends, goals, dreams, and worry—all calculated to help us forget anxiety, to feel important and loved.

What do you think is wrong with the children of

today? It's the same old snake in the grass, back with his new "grass," his heroin, his "crack," his strange herbal potions for injection into the vein, lung, brain, nose—every place you can think of—to produce a "high" that dulls the consciousness and makes the user feel invincible.

By one means or another: entertainment, religion, politics, medicine, music, drugs, and so on, the consciousness of man is gradually being numbed and destroyed. Man is becoming degenerate as his consciousness sinks *down* to new *highs*. Living it up is really dying, and one day, man's body and soul will reach their lowest level. On that day, as the soul arrives at the nadir of consciousness, and the body reaches the ultimate level of degeneration, sickness, and disease, the body disintegrates, and the soul crosses the border to meet its maker—and it's not the one you may think it is.

Life, then, is a movement up or down, through levels of consciousness, and if you haven't the strength to resist the daily pressures along the way, where will you get the strength to turn back from the border of Hell? You won't. If you are compulsive now in all your escape mechanisms, your petty indulgences, how can you ever resist the author of escape, your Hell God? You see, the loss of consciousness, once it starts, becomes a compulsive escape into the illusory reality of Hell that leads to Hell itself. Of course, this state of affairs can be changed by desire, but the downward-spiraling consciousness is compulsively hell-bound. Every time you err, fantasy rises to "save" your ego from the "sin" of knowing the Truth, and you fall another notch.

You cannot experience the kind of sorrow that will cleanse and change your nature until you wish with all your heart to come up out of your intellect into the Light of Realization. Your aim must not be to absorb, word for word, the facts written here, but to separate your conscious, aware self from its absorption in its thinking.

You will be ruled by pride as long as you live in the world of your imagination. No repentance or meaningful change will be available to you as long as you are content to live down there. Another reason you can not repent is that, down there, amid your worries, dreams and fantasies, you are cut off from Him whom you have offended. And there, lacking the understanding of what went wrong, you are tempted to try your hand at solving problems that only the Light can eradicate.

Lost in the false reality of your dream state, you can not find true life. Living in the dungeon of your mind, without the Light to warm and revive you, your soul is dying and your body is decaying. Information is nothing but *outformation*—that is to say, a way of life shaped by externally-triggered, demonic animal impulses. And your will, which is really no will at all because it is the tool of various impulses, you take to be your own chosen way. How can you see otherwise?

The tragedy of conscious life springs naturally from a misguided faith. Faith in anything, good or bad, determines the direction the soul takes and the way the body grows. As a result, every decision that is based on faith in a deception will cause you to end up 180 degrees from where you would have been if you had had true faith. You must know, for example, whether your child has a real need for something or is simply trying to get his own way—and the way you relate to that one simple situation can have a pronounced effect on the direction of both of your lives. And how can you expect to know such things unless you are aware and guided by a true faith?

Here is another example: If you are objective, you can see clearly how misguided others are. Since you can see what is controlling them, you can also see that they are not your enemy, but what controls them is. How can you be upset with them after you realize that? You will be patient with them, knowing that what is inside them wants you to react with resentment so that it can get inside you also. You won't doubt yourself when you realize this. You will stand firm in your faith.

Being objective about any matter enables you to see truly and to believe truly in what the light reveals to you. There is life in this knowing, and holding fast to knowing is faith. Faith is the basis of patience, and patience appears as a nonresponse to the world. It separates you from taking shape from evil as it joins you to God, who reveals things as they really are. Waiting in the shadow and watching for the first sign of your wavering is that other god, who causes you to read wrong meanings into everything and makes you react like a wind-up toy.

Alas for those of you who fail to see clearly. You believe falsely, and that false belief separates you from Reality. Up pops resentment and impatience with your fellow beings. A wrong grows up inside you that thrives on judgment and is ashamed of the Light. To feed that proud judgmental creature, you not only read non-existent meaning into situations, but you delight as well in all the bona fide wrongs you are bound to see because you are always on the lookout for them.

Everything that goes wrong with your life does so as the result of your misguided faith. Your emotions, fears, and guilts arise from a false faith that governs your outlook on what you believe is happening to you.

Even when you believe in the worst that is about to befall you—and you do so compulsively—you cannot make yourself disbelieve it. After all, you have become a creature who relies on proof, not faith, and all you can see is proof staring you in the face. Thanks to your misguided faith, you can believe only as the result of being deceived, so that even when you believe positively that all will be well, it's a lie, and you know it, but you have to cling to it.

The ego cannot know true life and faith in its fallen state. You must come up from the murky depths of the intellect to realize the Truth. Any effort to reverse a morbid belief results in more guilt, simply because the efforts exerted by ego involve you with thought. Your own attempts at reversing faith always backfire sooner or later, to intensify your morbid belief in death, the ultimate reward of the only belief possible in the state of pride.

Learning by rote what is written here cannot help you, any more than learning about the sun can give you a suntan. You must use the knowledge you find here in a very special way: to lead you to where the Light shines.

When you meditate, be sure that you are doing it correctly. Of course, you can't meditate correctly if your attitude is wrong, so you had better be ready to let

170

go of pride and "die to the world," in a manner of speaking. You can recognize a prideful attitude by the way a person under its control gets caught up in knowledge and has to study and rationalize everything he does. Haven't I said that pride can exist as pride only when it stays out of the Light? So if your attitude is not pure, your pride will not let you give yourself over to pure meditation, but will carry you away from the Light into a deep hypnotic state of fantasy—deeper than the one you were in prior to your attempt to use the meditation. So watch your sincerity, lest you wind up further from the Truth rather than closer to it.

The evidence that you are following the instructions correctly is that you will not be able to remember anything in the instructions verbatim, and yet you will be starting to understand the real nature of your problems, and they will begin to fall away as they lose their importance and morbid power over you. You will find yourself naturally making better decisions, becoming more patient, less ambitious. Any present sickness will start to disappear, while an old one that you thought had been cured might reappear in order to receive its proper treatment in the healing light of Reality.

Please bear in mind the principal use of this book, which is to teach you how to separate the "thinker" you from the prejudice of your thinking and return you to the real "You," the one you were born to be. Whatever else you read in these pages is there to witness to the way you are going, so don't struggle to learn any of it. Just observe, understand, be still, and know.

10 Ego Attitudes: Problems of Man-Woman Relationships

You will be terrified when you discover the truth in this text because it strikes to the heart of your blind, egosexual identity—the one you are trying so hard to be proud of. But if you will tighten your seat belt and hear me out, you might just find the solution to all your problems, and as a fringe benefit, the key you have been looking for to solve the whole riddle of existence.

By now, you know that I'm not going to hand you the same old line, the one that says "sex is love and life, and more of it is heaven and happiness." That is the kind of garbage you have been fed all your life. And you see where it got you: into the mess you're in right now, the one that drove you to look for better guidelines.

So let's look at the other side of the coin, the one that few dare examine. How often do you see anything that is critical of sex in print? Have you ever even seen the subject discussed intelligently? I think not. Until now.

But be careful! If you read me right, you will never be the same; you will change for better or worse. So if you don't want to know the Truth about your sexual origin, you might want to skip this chapter.

Has it ever occurred to you that drugs, booze, and

making love are all closely interrelated? Probably not; but it is true that all vices rise, one out of the other, as the result of our failure to deal correctly with the first one in the devolutionary chain. Every strange urge that rises from our failure to respond to a situation correctly is compounded by the way we toy with it. We react and we change, until we find it impossible to see beyond the symptoms of change to the cause itself. We are too caught up in the process of reinforcing the sin through repetition.

Do something you shouldn't and up rises a strange animal desire that will torment you until you yield to it. But when you do yield for relief, you feel torment again for having yielded. Do you see how all your troublesome compulsions—to drink, to smoke, to snort, to sex—bear evidence to your many failings on the downgrade?

You should not fall in love with your faults. If only you could see clearly that that is what you are doing, you might be less likely to abandon yourself mindlessly and passionately to their beckoning, as though you were engaged in some marvelous devotion. You should be able to dissolve any compulsion through passive observation of the conditioning that brought it about. If you can get your proud ego out of the way long enough to become perfectly objective in your observation, you should be able to see all the way back to the first cause, and when you do, you will see that it was the pride you inherited from Adam. It might not be so hard for you to see the truth of this when it comes to gambling, drinking, and "shooting up," but take another look at your attitude toward sex. If you equate sex with love, as most of us do before enlightenment, ask yourself whether you are not mistaking a failing for a virtue. Then question your other failings; see how they spring from the stubborn pride you take in sexuality, your number one failing. You must finally conclude, with me, that every vice you can imagine rises from the misuse of sex.

Certainly, sex is a natural thing for animals, but man is not an animal by nature, but by way of defaulting to nature—failing, in other words. He inherits his sexual identity through a mysterious flaw in his ego character, and that flaw is what I intend to explore with you in the following pages from every conceivable angle.

In my own case, for instance, the reason I am not turned on and excited by women is that I can see clearly how that way of relating to women is harmful to them and works to their disadvantage. Most men can't. They are too busy with thoughts of *taking* advantage.

Of course, imagining that you are going to derive some personal benefit from a situation is the very thing that makes any wrong attractive and exciting to the ego. In the end, though, instead of getting, you get got!

Your only protection against deception in all its forms is the gift of seeing things clearly—all the way to the end—before you get involved with them. In the following pages, I hope to expose the tricks deceivers use in order to control your life. To do so, I have to start at the beginning, at the source of all human problems: the man-woman relationship.

When you are not fully committed to what you know is right deep down in your heart, then you are loyal to every rotten thing that pulls on you. This failure to "bond" with Principle fairly well explains compulsion and all the suffering, guilt, and terror it gives rise to. When your ego attitude is wrong, you see evil as good. It seems to serve you, but all it does is enslave you. And as the illicit feelings and desires, and the symptoms they create, rise—you fall. Now, you can do one of two things: you can look at your compulsion, see it for what it is, and let it pass; or you can see it as normal and revel in it, milking it for all the sensual thrill it can give you. In which direction are you leaning? Your answer will be a measure of your devotion to the truth in your heart.

For the sake of our salvation, we must reexamine, understand, and perhaps reexperience the way we have failed—not by some psychological, intellectual standard or thought process, but by the very Light from which we have fallen as the result of falling into our minds in our search for answers to life's riddles. Ideally, of course, you should come to realize your need for a new orientation while you are still involved with the partner you have been using to serve your ego, the one you are beginning to see as your seductive and threatening slave driver.

You must begin by recognizing that ancient sin for what it is, because it is responsible for your descent into a sensuous, sexual being. When it happened to Adam, he looked upon himself "and he was ashamed, because he saw he was naked." He suddenly became self-conscious when he became aware of the alteration in his nature and knew in his heart that the alteration was not for the better.

Understand, then, that sexuality is not our sin so

much as it is the evidence of Adam's sin. We have inherited our sex-death-animal identity from that first man, whose pride made him vulnerable to the serpent-inspired offering of the woman. In spite of all the centuries that have passed since then, man is still self-conscious where sex is concerned, and that is the way he should very well be.

Because of their inherited pride, men look at women primarily with sexual longing, the evidence of pride's failing. But we who share the legacy of death are now sinning by compulsion rather than choice, and by reveling in sexual activity, we unconsciously reinforce the pride that led to our fall to sexuality in the first place.

Our fallen, sensual bodies do not answer willingly to Reason, but to the woman, who has inherited the power to trigger man's desire for her, as well as for anything that man sees as being connected with her in some way. The longer we live, the more conditioned we become to the female form. And when sex is practiced as an escape from anxiety, it arouses other animal feelings and desires in us. If we practice sex as a kind of escape, a means of emptying ourselves of guilt in order to know innocence again, we do so because of the pride that caused us to degenerate in the first place. We fall prey, not only to sex, but to other lowly animal desires and the anxieties they bring with them. We fall in love with our own sensuality. We react to all our impulses as we do to sex. We indulge ourselves in them, trying to find relief from anxiety by running from Reality.

On reaching maturity, a youth arrives at the state of being that Adam came down to know, and, like Adam, he reacts to the mystery with the same shame. Not knowing the reason for it, and not knowing how to cope with the burning and awkwardness of his sexuality, he tries to lose himself in the source of his embarrassment as a way of dealing with the anxiety it causes him.

Today's man, generations removed from Adam's firsthand and direct knowledge of Truth, nevertheless experiences the same anxiety as he approaches the threshold of Light from which man fell in the beginning. And he commits the same sin by escaping into the images of his mind and the reinforcing, ego-building love of the female.

Because you are a man, your ego instinctively reacts against the Light, as though the Light were the enemy. And then you find refuge, first, in fantasy, and then, in the reassurance of many sensual experiences, from which the sin self grows and cries out to be loved. Even the terrible sin of murder results from an anguished soul's attempt at self-expression. Any impulse that is painful to observe and almost impossible to repress will cause you to seek relief by indulging, and escaping into, it.

All of our problems are so centered in sexuality that our sexual conditioning leads inexorably to all the lower levels of degeneration. But it is Pride that forms the foundation of our crumbling house. It is Pride that causes our ego to be so dead-set against seeing any form of evidence pointing to its sinfulness. It therefore seeks acceptance for its faults just the way they are.

While Adam's sin was the rejection of Reality, yours is an unwillingness to face up to it, and as long as you hold this attitude, your problems grow in the dark soil of your sensuality and guilt. Meanwhile, your temptress changes her role in your relationship. First, a willing lover and entertainer, she gradually becomes your executioner.

As a rule, a man is first seduced through his mind, but after that, his body takes over as the site of entry. Women, on the other hand, develop their power over men through their bodies at an early age. Later, they acquire a formidable power over their children. Any man who refuses to wake from his sexual trance must sooner or later pay with his life. After all, the wages of sin (enjoying, rather than rejecting it) is death.

Man's first sin, pride, the desire to be his own god, soon led to its expression in the physical world as sexuality, the root of all our worldly problems. You may not see the role pride has played in your sexuality, but how about *ambition*, pride's right-hand expression? The ambitious man not only develops a vast cornucopia of desires, things he wants so badly he can taste them, but he wants to feel perfectly entitled to go after them by any means at his disposal. Is there a better means to this end than the support of a woman?

A man's prideful ambition leads irrevocably to his putting sex first, and the woman herself, second. Everything he does is motivated by his sexual drive and his ego's need to feel secure through sexual acceptance.

Man has expressed his proud ambition through his sex drive from the beginning of time; but if he can take another look at it—honestly and from a more objective angle—he need not compound the guilt of it. If he can look at his desires honestly, he can see how he has been using sex as a means of supporting the deeper sin of prideful ambition. The guilt of being too ambitious has led him to seek comfort in the prideful use of the woman's body for reassurance, for somehow making the wrong right. Now, if he can see clearly how he fell into the pit, and be genuinely sorry about it, he will find his first toehold on the upward climb to freedom and dignity.

Lust, the lowest from of sexuality, represents the ego's stubborn refusal to deal with sex in its milder expressions. In his pride, a man insists on seeing all his failings as virtues. He must believe that the deceived self is the true self, so he looks at women in a funny way, a way that telegraphs his excitement over her presence, and at the same time, begs her to support his pride by validating his sexual sensitivity to temptation. Alas, this way of looking at a woman can have a mysterious and dangerous effect on her mind.

An ambitious female tends to look for that hungry look, because it signals an easy mark, a weak, ambitious mama's boy, who can be used by his use of her. Nothing excites and inflates the ego of a woman more than a weak, needful man. How it excites her proud "need to be needed!" And all young men interpret that hungry excitement as "love" for them. What fools we mortals be!

If you will look at yourself closely, you will see that all your problems are growing from the same ground: your philosophical outlook, the way you believe. It is your belief that determines your aim, your goal, your direction in life, up or down, the kind of people you draw to you to support your goals first, and later the strange faults and needs that you develop along the way.

The way you look at women, the way you fixate on your sexuality as your center, reveals a selfish stubbornness, a way of looking on a woman's love as the

180

way to manhood and to glory. Can you see the connection between pride and sexuality? Can you see how your pride's insistence on getting what it wants in life, and wanting to be right in its wrong wants, leads to your seeking reinforcement through sexual stimulation with the wrong kinds of women? Or worse yet, with women you *make* wrong to serve you. Your attitude determines the kind of friends you will draw to you. It will also determine your choice of a mate, and what you will bring out of the woman you select. The quality of the love you extend to "your" woman will prove itself out in experience. If it is the wrong kind—strictly the product of sexual longing—it will turn into violence, hate, and contempt.

At a certain point in your ego-sexual career, you are bound to notice that it has led inexorably to two standard situations:

(1) Your wife becomes unreasonable. She take liberties in what you consider (rightly or wrongly) to be your own domain, and you have no control over her at all. If these words don't describe your wife, take a good look in the mirror; they may apply to you. Sex and upmanship go together like salt and pepper, or bread and butter. If you have elected not to marry, you may find that you have been hooked, totally dominated, by one woman after another—you just can't win for losing.

(2) You feel a growing anxiety, a growing need to prove yourself through sexual love. The sexual love you have been indulging for your ego's sense of security has somehow become the cause of your *insecurity*. It has lost some of its turn-on value. You may even become impotent, unable to rise to the demands of a

clinging woman you once *taught,* in your foolishness, to want and welcome your sexuality.

Remember all I have said concerning failing: sexual feelings are rooted in your proud need to escape Reality. Pride, being wrong, never wants to face the fact that it is wrong. So, in the devolutionary spiral into mortality, wrong expresses itself, first, as a natural sex drive, then as lust, and finally in a smorgasbord of needs, drives, and fears. Lust represents the stubbornness of the ego that refuses to face Reality and insists on being worshipped as a sexual god. It becomes completely involved in the nature it should be observing, instead of wallowing in, over and over again. The more gross a person becomes, the more proud he is of his rottenness.

You have probably already discovered how impossible it is to break a habit before you see that it is wrong, by a cold, clear, unimpassioned seeing. There is a certain magic in the calm seeing of wrong as wrong that empowers it to conquer the wrong it is observing. You will never get to see the mystery beyond, the *why* of it, until you have first dissolved the overt symptom of your fall by the Light of Reality. In other words, we are often able to cure a symptom before we understand the spiritual failing that caused it, but only if we love the truth enough to see the symptom for what it is, without trying to escape from knowing we are wrong. After the habit has given us up, and we see that we are no longer reacting emotionally to the situations that used to trigger it, we do arrive at a deeper understanding of the causative factor, and we are ready to do battle with the next fault. Sexuality, insofar as it is "normal" to our animal nature, will probably be one of the last sins we will overcome, but we should certainly be able to start dealing with the sins of imagery and lust.

When Adam's ego came down into the earthy, intellectual state of pride, it was automatically cut off from the principled, paradisaical state of eternity through self-renewal. It was no longer a part of the system of perpetuation through inner regeneration. Now, it had to perpetuate itself, like any "other" mammal, through sexual generation, the making of new bodies as opposed to making bodies new. We projections of Adam have inherited the proclivity of pride that is locked into sexual self-expression and ends in death. Pride forces you to express yourself in sexual terms, to see sex as "love," but seeing sex as "love" always changes sex to lust, causing man to become a sexual junkie, and woman a hooker.

All men feel a mysterious awkwardness about their sex drives; but they soon see that one way of getting "on top" of something that seems to be part of you and that you can't shake, is to take pride in it, and they do. That is what causes them to look at women in that special way, with lust and longing. As for the recipient of that look, being cast in the role of mistress or entertainer affects a woman in a way that is harmful to her, even though she might find it to be pleasant and flattering in the beginning. Her first response to the weak man she attracts is therefore likely to be a reinforcing of the wrong in both of them as her own sick ego need rises to fulfill his.

The animal lust of a woman flatters the male and causes him to give her the starring role in their drama, and as her ego delights in this unexpected stardom, her self-image rises to glorious heights and causes her to degrade herself in the name of genuine love, for that is what she thinks she feels. The sick part of a woman's nature wants the man's animal wrongness to lust after her, cry out to her, because his weakness gives her strength. She revels in feeling sorry for him and answering his needs like an angel from heaven. And of course, in time, both male and female become somewhat sated with their ego-sexual use of each other—enough so, at least, to realize that some of their other ego needs are being threatened with starvation as the result of their having been so long preoccupied with making the maximum use of their sexual opportunities. He realizes that his love for the woman has caused him to lose the grip of authority over certain areas that he assumed to be vested in him by reason of his being the man of the house. She, on the other hand, is beginning to feel entitled to having some say in the household decision-making process, and he sees her efforts in this direction as "taking liberties." Of course, this little game of "upmanship" has been going on from day one, under cover of the romantic surface, each one trying to jockey his own assumptions about what his role should be into the number one spot. He has been "buying" sexual considerations by gradually letting go of the leadership he feels entitled to, while she has been buying leadership by giving him more control over her sex life than she thinks the marriage contract entitles him to have.

Now, when the man wakes up to his diminished authority, and seeks to get it back by correcting his wife, he is horrified to discover that he has made a god of her, thus setting her above his power to control or correct. If he wants to continue having sex and ego support, he will have to continue paying for it with the coin of his manly prerogatives. He certainly doesn't want to see that, from the woman's point of view, he has been "taking liberties" with her body, and that as far as she is concerned, it's just a case of "tit for tat." What a stalemate! And we're all headed that way, thanks to our slimy little undercover maneuvering for ascendancy.

One would think that, all things being equal, a man and a woman could sit down before marriage and forestall this impasse by defining their roles and expectations in advance, and negotiating a relationship that will be acceptable to both. On the surface, one would think so, but those who are caught in the undercurrent of romantic involvement have little inclination to come up to reality. Furthermore, all things are not always equal between them.

Where sexual hunger is concerned, there is usually a quantitative difference between the sexes—at least, over the long haul. And when it comes to spirituality, or innocence, there is a qualitative difference. Men are seldom aware of this difference, and it is certainly the last thing today's woman "libber" wants to see! But even the most militant "libber" should be able to observe that most women expect to be more fairly treated by a male than a female boss; they seem to have an instinctive fear of their fellow woman's worldly guilefulness. They might not agree with me when I say that this instinctive knowledge of how to manipulate a man to get what they want (or to go to his jugular when they fail) is an inheritance from Eve, the first woman, but they should be able to admit that it is a force to be reckoned with in their fellow woman, even if they can't see it in themselves. If they do see their own proclivity for roundabout, not-quite-honest dealing, they might just see it as the underdog's way of compensating for the lack of real power, but see it they must. Of course, there exists here and there a woman who has escaped Eve's curse, even as there exists here and there a man who has escaped Adam's, but they don't need me, so I must address myself to those who are still looking for the road to salvation. (Naturally, it won't harm the innocent ones to read along, if only to learn what they are up against in the world.)

The fact is that the original metaphysical sin behind the sexual contract continues to duplicate and compound itself on lower and lower carnal levels. Originally, the man taught (or allowed, by reason of his lacking the corrective power of love) woman to tempt him to be ambitious and prideful. Today, this default of divine love expresses itself in his abuse of her, his using her as a sexual object rather than correcting her from that role.

Let me restate the principle in a different way:

If I tempt you to become a thief, you might actually become a thief. Now, as a thief, your consciousness will be different from that of an honest person. You will also have a different nature, and it will cause you conflict because it doesn't agree with the one you had before you were tempted. Now there are two ways to deal with the anxiety resulting from your wrongdoing:

(1) You can admit the error and return to your

former state, or

(2) You can look to your tempter for reinforcement of the excitement and pleasure you felt when you first fell under his spell. When he sees your longing look, he might be more than happy to oblige you, knowing that he is the god of your changed self and will stay in control as long as you look to him for satisfaction. This feeling of power, of being needed, is what a female looks for as the basis of her ego security. You, the man in this little allegory, will have to content yourself with whatever pleasure and delusion you can garner from your fall to temptation.

So, without realizing the nature of her need, which is basically to destroy the man for life and power, a woman will nurture the wrong in him. She sustains him in his prideful state, which results in making him more unprincipled than ever—also, more lustful and guilty. His lust fans life into the potential demon of hell that lurks in the female soul, and like a black widow spider, it proceeds to devour the man who roused it to life. Strangely enough, being eaten alive by a *femme fatale* doesn't set off the alarm in a man that being eaten by a shark would; on the contrary, men love the savage hell they call up out of their women to service their lustfulness. It's much more exciting to love the hell *in* a woman than it is to love it *out* of her.

No man in his gross failing state ever really loves the woman for herself. He loves the creeping serpent self that he wakes in her to feed, and feed *on*, his passion, his fall from human dignity. The woman discovers that she is being forced to support something less than human, a rat, for what she loves is just a projection of her own private hell, crying to her to at least be a happy rat. That is why she finds it so hard to resist the poor rat. After all, he *is* her child, no matter what—a pathetic, baby demon-god, crying out to his mother/father god.

A woman rarely gives sex for the sake of her own sexual pleasure, but for the mental relief of guilt or pressure, and for that elusive thing called "security." The ultimate need of a woman is not for sex, much as a man would have it otherwise, but for correction. Instead of being "loved" *into* it, she has an unrecognized yearning to be loved *out* of that naughty sexual role.

A man capable of compassionate love will develop a diminishing need to cry to a woman and to excite her maternal feelings for him. In fact, he will become a dreadful bore, with his superior love and stoic non-response to the blandishments of an unregenerate Eve.

True love *never* seeks a reward for its loving. It is simply a fact of life for the consciousness in which it resides. The person who gets excited in the presence of a person he expects to be serving him some exciting feelings is really thinking only of himself, his own pleasure. He is completely selfish, and the woman who has excited his amorous feelings knows that she is being used, not loved.

Many women bemoan the fact that their husbands are drunken, unprincipled cads; yet when you ask them whether they were aware of these weaknesses before they got married, they have to answer with a sheepish "yes." Of course, they are quick to add that they got married for security, a true answer, but not a very nice one.

For a season, even seeking women are often just as ignorant of their natural heritage as most men want to be. They often play coy games to cement a man's woman-created need for them, once they see the potential for its further development in that special look of waking lust. But not all women go along with this game out of guilefulness. Some of them harbor an understandable hope that it might somehow lead them to true love later on. All too often, that hope turns to bitterness when the woman discovers that the man has no intention of outgrowing his need for her, but rather intends to go on using her forevermore.

What a woman really needs from a man, and what forms the basis for her future security in the bottom of her heart, is for him to grow up. She might not be able to put words to her longing, but it is to see his ego mature to the point of being able to question the way he has been relating to her. She is actually suffering from his encouraging the wrong in her, loving her only for her wrongness and rejecting her when she is right enough to see him for what he really is.

Sex, then, is not love. Sex is sex, just as eating is eating and going to the toilet is going to the toilet. You can make more out of these things, but you are not right in the head when you do.

Sex is man's need for God gone wrong, misdirected. A man can not possibly see the Truth as long as his ego is worshipfully involved with sex as love; and sex as love is the only love a vain ego wants to have anything to do with. The hallowing of the wrong relationship between two fallen beings casts a rosy glow over their sin and makes it look innocent. But in the Light of Reality, sex love (mutual worship) is a falling away from True Love.

Look at the facts: there are two loves, two human needs, to be exact. One of them is to be loved as though you were a god, which leads to a sex need that requires sexual loving. The other need, the true need, is to be loved by being corrected from sensual needs. A man needs to realize the truth about sex for himself, and the woman needs him to do so, for he won't stop using her until he does.

Do you see how a woman's need to be loved can compel a man to fall from reason to worship her? When a man falls, they both fall into what they think is "love," but is sex, complete with all the weird feelings and failings that go with it.

Can you see how a man's sexual lust represents his refusal to face Reality, and how it can excite a woman's ego with feelings of power? Male lust is complimentary to the pride of some women, but it is an abomination to the more sensible women who are looking for a man, not a dog.

I am not suggesting that you should give up sex. On the contrary, you should learn how to practice it correctly. What I am saying is that every woman has an unrecognized need to be degraded in order to gain power for her ego. Behind this secret wish lurks a devilish desire to become a dominant mother to the man, and that is exactly what she becomes when the man falls for it. But if he were able to practice sex in a non-ego-supporting way, the real love that enabled him to do so would throw a bucket of cold water on the woman's guile and leave her chastened by a goodly shame. Continuing to practice sex incorrectly, of course, results in increasing the woman's need for sex as the token of love, but it is a love that never leads to real satisfaction.

A man looks longingly at a pretty woman because his ego unconsciously fixates to her as though she were a missing part of himself; and I suppose she is, in a sense. The more beautiful she is, the more he desires to have her fill the void in his being. He sees her as a missing part of himself only because of a trick of temptation that steals his life away while seeming to fulfill it. It is a vicious cycle, and it goes something like this:

The more he tries to fulfill himself from her, the more of himself seems to migrate to her, creating a larger void in himself that keeps crying out for the lost identity that beckons to him from its new home in her, challenging him to come and get it back. Does it not seem strange to you that a person can actually acquire, or even want to acquire, the essence of another person? What kind of love is it that wants to appropriate a part of another person's beingness? Surely it is the perversion of our need for God that arises through our need to identify ourselves as Him.

The entire function of a female vanity is to draw so much of a man's attention to herself that he becomes utterly preoccupied with her, and can no longer see, let alone do, what he ought to be doing with his life. Of course, the vain man doesn't mind this state of affairs one bit, because as long as his attention is riveted on her, he can forget how wrong he is.

Now, if you can understand all the forces operating within a woman, you can appreciate the kind of love she really needs. But if you fail as a man, by means of

191

your sexual fixations, to find the understanding you need in order to relate properly to a woman, the hell in her will drag both of you to your graves.

In her monstrous quest for attention, a woman can make her children hate their father in order to get them to cling to her with a greater need for her love. And through her power to diminish a man (by degrading herself and offering herself as an easy sexual tidbit), she can easily upset him to bring out his violence and weakness in front of the children, thereby showing them how bad their father is in comparison with their wonderful mother.

You must give a woman the right kind of attention, the right kind of love, because if you give her the wrong kind, the kind that gives you too much pleasure, you will give her your power along with the attention. Whenever you give her attention, and she returns love for it, you drive each other up the wall, first, with delight, and then, with frustration.

A compulsive, fixated attention is no substitute for an attention given freely, with genuine interest and love for the woman herself. Men are fascinated with women because the only love they have to give them is a failing love. Their extreme hypnotic fixation is the result of their having fallen away from Love and Reason. Men use temptation as a way to forget the beastly changes that temptation has wrought in them.

So, this whole process of "natural" love exposes what is going on inside us; and in a way, it proves the existence of God by proving the existence of evil. It is very hard for a lustful man to resist a female lure. The excitement of her sexual presence has an effect on him that is similar to the emotion of resentment, in that it forces him to give in to it in order to relieve the emotional pressure, and then look at his giving in as love.

Resentment is to anger as sex is to lust. Resentment is the ego's way of reexperiencing the natural evidence of failing, anger, in order to avoid seeing it for the inferior animal weakness it is. Again, that is not to say that we should never react with anger, but that we should see it as the weakness it is.

A man would never know lust if he were able to look honestly and questioningly at his sexual desire, and see that it represents his inferiority to woman, instead of escaping into it as the means of seeing nothing beyond his own gratification. When he gives in to lust for the woman who excites and accepts it in him, he forgets that it is a weakness, not a strength.

It is impossible to continue to do something wrong, once you are fully aware of what you are doing. Awareness modifies behavior patterns, upgrades them. Through awareness, we are enabled to defer the gratification of our natural desires to appropriate times, instead of indulging them on the spot, when we see that they are out of step with the total situation. Through awareness, a man can resume control of his life and correct his relationship with the woman with whom he shares it. If he has turned her into a witch, he will find the strength to turn out the witch in favor of the woman who might have been waiting to be discovered and valued for herself.

11 Sex: The Substitute Love

The person who loves the Truth has a ground to receive it. He has been graced to know the good seed from the bad, and will therefore reject the latter; he is not easily deceived. The prideful person, on the other hand, is so grounded in deception as his standard that he falls easily into error and can never see where he went wrong.

A woman shows her love through cooperation with the loved person, but if she has chosen to love a vain, sensual, lustful man, her cooperation only brings out the worst in both of them. So what can she do? The answer lies, not so much in *what* to do, but in understanding how the wrong values are being transmitted and reinforced in the "doing."

The woman usually ends by resenting the man as a way of dealing with him and his faults, but resentment makes her feel guilty, and the guilt makes her want to cooperate with him more, both as a means of making up for the guilt and as a way to get him to yield up more of that illusive thing called "love." To him, of course, and perhaps even to her, that "love" is sex. And the sex he gives her in the name of love only encourages the wrong in her to cooperate with the wrong in him, again and again. It is a vicious cycle.

A wife's best defense is to become less eager to please her husband until he changes, while taking care not to resent him for his failure to do so. A single woman's best defense is to look for a principled man in the first place, rather than settle for the one whose weakness is so exciting to her. She must disabuse herself of the notion that her supportive love is a magic wand that will fulfill and make a better man of him.

Service is the magic wand of the devil, his favorite way of gaining dominion over his victims. The uncorrected woman uses service to gain power, but the stronger she gets, the more contempt she feels for the weakling she serves. So it is that the weak man, whose ego cries out to be serviced, feeds a woman with a false sense of security and noblesse in the beginning, and bitter contempt in the end.

Every young woman should test for a very special quality in the man she plans to marry. She should make sure that he loves what is *right* more than he loves her. And that kind of man should look for a woman who is willing to be corrected by him. When both these considerations are met, all ego conflicts between husband and wife are easily resolved and they live happily ever after.

The sensible woman seeks a rare and special kind of love, one that few men are capable of giving. She wants to be loved as a person, for her potential as a partner, quite aside from any sexual attractiveness she may, or may not, possess. She is not interested in playing guileful little games to "get her man," but if she has wanted to marry badly enough to have resorted to them (how else could she get a man's attention?) she will know that she has chosen wisely if her chosen man loves her enough in that nonsexual way to discourage her from playing the traditional guileful games. She will breathe a sigh of relief when he stands as a correction to those "womanly" ways. Simply by looking at them in a brotherly, nonjudgmental way, *and failing to fall for them*, he causes her to feel the shame of them herself. Furthermore, she knows that she can safely let go of them now, for she has found the security of real love.

A man of understanding, who loves what is right more than the woman herself, is soon able to consider her real needs over and above his own selfish ones. Consequently, he is able to resolve the feelings that would otherwise compel him to feed her madness and abuse her in the usual way.

Of course, not all "considerate" men are sincere. Witness the crafty lover, the selfish dog, who tiptoes around his woman so carefully, is so careful not to offend, and so considerate of her feelings—all with one end in mind: the ego support that he needs to support his pride. The rogue simply *has* to love her "just the way she is," in order to get her to accept, sustain, and please *him* "just the way *he* is."

A man who loves a woman more than anything in the world, more even than God, is on one big ego trip, on his way to becoming an unprincipled selfish beast. Unless a man's soul yearns to know and to do what is right in his heart, before anything else, he will never be blessed with the secret Godly knowledge that will make him master of his home and a good husband and father.

What does a naughty child need above all else? Surely it is correction from being naughty. A self-correcting child is rare; he needs a principled, patient father to love the hell out of him (the hell that was planted in him by his devious, confusing mother). Alas, most husbands and fathers are too weak to stand up to the stresses of their naughty wives and children. They either become violent to relieve the pressure, or they give in and give up. Some of them become workaholics in order to have an excuse to stay away from the atmosphere of contempt that surrounds them at home.

Compare an exciting woman with a naughty child. She is sexually exciting only because she is "naughty." If she is ever to become the real woman God intended her to be, she will have to be corrected from the female state. But if a man does not understand this, he will respond to her with the usual pattern of failing that accompanies sexual yielding, and he will come into heat with her. His surrender to sex, his animal love in lieu of real love, encourages the female guile to rise up and take over. When a woman feels cheated out of true life by a man's selfish use of her, she takes the reins resentfully, and wreaks a terrible revenge with the coin of contempt.

By its very nature, a man's imperious sex drive encourages his wife to be naughty, and the naughtier she gets, the more exciting she gets. So he falls again and again. When the process gets to the point that it is revolting, even to him, impotence sets in. His failing, his unchallenged need, has brought out the worst in his wife and has caused her to keep sweetening the bait in order to remain the basis of his comfort. But how comfortable does a man deserve to be? After all, Adam was completely unaware of his sexuality until after he had disobeyed his Creator, so it isn't very likely that he was being "rewarded" for his disobedience. Is it not more of a penance, a big stumbling block for him to overcome on the road to salvation? (Even if you don't take the story of the Garden at face value, you must surely agree that it reeks of poetic justice and forms a good psychological basis for the continuing conflict, internal as well as external, both within and between men and women. At least, it deserves a second look.)

One part of your child, the naughty part, wants its own way. And if he succeeds in getting it, he will "love" you for giving in, thus making you feel "rewarded" for your failing. And what is true of the child is equally true of the immature, uncorrected, culturally-altered woman—the female who is not yet woman. However, there is another side to the woman, as well as to the child, that cries out for you to oppose and overpower the wicked dark side of her nature. Has your child never asked you, loudly enough to be overheard by an impatient playmate, "You did ask me to be home by 8 o'clock, didn't you, Dad?" We all have a rarely seen quality that cries out silently to be touched by true love; but in the case of women, this marvelous side has been overwhelmed by an evil nature that revels in the power she derives from rewarding some man for his failing.

When boy meets girl, he automatically uses any naughtiness he sees in her to sustain the naughtiness in himself. He falls for her, and she likes the feeling—at least, at first. Remember here that men who refuse to face the truth either "love" their women *into* being wrong or *for* being wrong. Similarly, many weak fathers enjoy the acceptance of the children they have spoiled rotten through their wicked weakness. When a man is wrong, he will set up an evil to accept him as right. The compulsion to do so forms the basis of all dictatorships, sexual or social; it also goes far to explain our enslavements and addictions.

Every spoiled child "loves" (craves with secret loathing) the father who has corrupted him with his permissiveness. Conversely, the spoiled child furnishes the father with the secret value he derives from actually *using* the child's wickedness as the basis for a belief in himself. They pat each other's backs and go down together. In the same way, all weak men encourage, even to the point of worship, the evil in women, simply because they need what is wrong to sustain their stupid egos in their delusions of grandeur.

The proud male suffers from feelings of insecurity because he is not a real man. He therefore has a desperate need to prove to himself that the sexual identity he has taken on is actually the true man, rising to glory. He must feel that every need he degenerates to experience is the highest good there is; consequently, he must find some female lowlife who will pretend to enjoy his filthy expressions of love, for a price.

Nevertheless, sexual highs always represent new lows, the low being the point at which the truth about yourself and your playmate tries to dawn on you, but you won't let it in. It is the time when your male ego rejects the convicting Truth of the Holy Spirit in favor of the lying guile in the female who is rising to the occasion of your ego's need.

Every woman/child needs a special kind of fatherly love, the kind that knows when to give in as well as when *not* to give in. Not all of a child's demands are unreasonable, any more than it is always unreasonable for a woman to resist some sexual pressure. It could be untimely, and it very often is. It therefore behooves a man to know what is natural and what is lustful, what is in its natural season and what is an excessive indulgence in sensuality. He should be the one to decide the time and place, but his decisions in this regard must be so thoroughly grounded in what is right and reasonable and wise for both of them that a woman's guile has no space in which to function. If he is always ready and eager, like a cat at a mouse hole, the guile in a woman soon lets her know that she is the one in charge; she can therefore manipulate his hunger, and the satisfaction thereof, to get anything she wants. She may even feel that she has earned anything she gets in this way, considering the wear and tear on her sexual apparatus. Under these conditions, even when a man sees how shabbily he is being used, he is powerless to do anything about it because he has traded his authority for sexual gratification. He can not correct his wife until he becomes correct himself. Until then, every sexual episode will license and empower his wife to do anything she wants, however unreasonable it may be. It is a fate "worse than death," and in a way it does lead to the death of his soul, but he has brought it on himself.

Under no conditions should a man and a woman promote each other's appetites in order to gratify an ego need for entertainment. The nature of such a need is never *ever* love; in a man, it is a demand for escape from anxiety through indulgence, and in a woman, it is the hunger for a security feeling she derives from the man's power.

Normal women care very little for sex, and those who do have strong sex drives turn out to be more masculine than feminine. A man would do well not to confuse a woman's desire to please, her searching for true love beyond the sexual phase of marriage, with what seems to be a strong need for sex on her part. Some women pretend to have strong drives, but they may be sexually aggressive only because they are afraid their marriages will fall apart if they stop knuckling under to their weak, vicious husbands and giving them what they want. Women need both kinds of love, but they need Divine Love more than the other. That is to say, they will gladly give their bodies for the one as long as there is hope of finding the other, the true love, at the end of the road. God help the stubborn man who continues to use his wife only for pleasure, and has the audacity to call it "love."

Male babies are already hungry little animals when they come into the world, whereas girls, unless they are violated early in life, tend to be quite innocent and angelic by nature. But once a young girl's maidenhead, or hymen, has been ruptured, and she is initiated into the animal world of men, she becomes almost dependent on a man to find her way to God. She is no longer free to go her own way. Depending on the man's own maturity, he can lead the way to salvation for both of them, or he can block it—and for a season he probably will. The male enters the world already lustful in nature, almost compelled to corrupt a woman in order to get her to share his lusty orientation. He must join with a woman on a sexual basis, and experience the hell of his failing with her, before he wakes from his sleep and accepts his divine responsibility for the relationship with his Eve.

In the beginning, however, in the excitement of sexual discovery, a certain amount of deterioration takes place. A man conjures up a variety of filthy antics for the woman to perform, degrading her in the process, to obtain the relief he needs, not only for the sexual pressure, but for his anxiety concerning it. Because of his anxiety, he seldom chooses an honest and virtuous woman. Such a woman makes a man feel beastly, awkward, and guilty; but a guileful woman, who is lower on the scale of life and guiltier than he is, makes him feel alive and "innocent" again. Her lack of conflict about what they are doing to each other makes everything seem right and natural. She seems to be ready for anything at all, so all he has to worry about is his ability to fulfill her expectations. He enjoys the illusion of innocence for a season, but when the excitement wears off, anxiety returns and the cycle begins again. He has to find some new way to virtue through sex; so the woman must lower herself still more in order to excite him and give him a new high. Of course, every new high reinforces his sexual needfulness, and when it is accepted as "love," it results in more failing on his part, and loathing on hers.

Sexual pleasure allows a beast man to remain oblivious to his failings, but it tends to make a woman more conscious of hers, more aware of the pain and futility involved in its constant expression. Many women develop feelings of insecurity about their sexual performance and their need to please a man in that way in order to keep him "happy." But as long as they cooperate with, and serve, the something that they sense has gone wrong with their man, the men continue on their not-so-merry way. The woman's failure to sound the alarm constitutes a temptation in itself, and the pain inherent in any temptation has the power either to awaken a man to his failing or deepen his sleep. One way or another, a woman will destroy any man who persists in using her.

Women are extremely alert to the sexual failing of men, because they feel that it is their job to recognize it and use it to keep the men asleep. Girls are able to realize what it is that boys don't want to see about themselves, and when they grow to womanhood, they suffer more than men do as the result of that realization. Like a bartender, they must remain sober for the sake of the drunk. How else can they serve the poor drunk's need?

Of course, the average woman feels the need of a relationship with a man, but unless she plays the sex game in the beginning, she can hardly hope to have one at all. So a seeking woman cultivates her womanly wiles for the sake of acquiring a family and home, hoping that some day she will also know the true love that must lie beyond sex. The problem is that the sexual relationship makes him less of a man and more of a beast, and at the same time, stimulates her to tease him more artfully. So he falls into perpetual lust, and her dreams of true love are doomed to perpetual frustration.

The woman who is conscious of Reality, who has not escaped from the knowledge of what is happening to her, is conscious of the contempt she feels toward the man's total absorption in sexuality. She feels her resentment growing as her hopes fade, and she feels cheated out of genuine love. She may continue to cooperate sexually just in case she has misjudged the situation, but as time goes by and she sees that she is being used more and loved less, she grows vengeful.

In their desperation, some women seek the love they long for in other men, but these eager creeps are no more capable of real love than the man they have cuckolded. They simply encourage her to play the role of a lower animal, and as she continues to share in the greater guilt of the man, she often takes the full blame on herself. As a result, she might at some times attribute her guilt feelings to her failure to perform well enough to please him. As she tries harder, she derives some relief from his pleasure with her. Obviously, the man has been training her to be a better whore, and he has been a cruel teacher, for she now tries to compensate for her guilt feelings by being a good little student and putting his pleasure above all other goals. Now she knows utter futility, as she is committed to using animal love as compensation for the true love she once sought. She may develop an insatiable need for sex in order to escape the guilt of resentment that rises to her consciousness, unbidden, in each sexual encounter. She is locked in the vicious cycle of looking for the cure in the sickness.

A woman's guilt stems partly from being degraded, and partly from the resentment she feels for being cheated out of true love. She tries to use the animal love of a man to quell the fires of anxiety that accompany it, but she is torn by ambivalence. Her eagerness for real love runs on a parallel track with the bitterness she feels toward the only kind of love a man ever offers. For a woman, sex can become a way of relieving the guilt she feels for resenting her husband's sexual abuse—it isn't the sex she wants, so much as the relief of guilt. It's like drinking to relieve the guilt of drinking. She requires a great deal of emotional excitement to relieve her mental anguish, so it will seem as though she is enjoying the sex, whereas her real relief is from the emotional anxiety.

The high that a woman feels when she cooperates sexually with a man is not so much sexual as it is *associated* with sex. It blows her mind clean, and it helps her to forget the lows to which she has been sinking.

In the process of living out of a man's essence (his failing), a woman can develop the sensitivity of her clitoris to such a degree that she can climax like a man; but when she does, she is in danger of "becoming" a man. When she becomes aggressive, the man becomes shy and retiring. He may even become impotent and lose interest in sex, like a woman. At last, he finds out what it's like to be a woman and get chased all the time.

Weak, insecure, egotistical men crave female sexual aggression; they are terribly offended if the female fails to climax with them. They want the craving they feel for the woman to be reciprocated by her, and to the same degree. That way, they are less threatened by the loss of control. Such a man needs this relationship in order to overcome the growing inferiority he feels in respect to the woman he has "conquered," the woman who is actually conquering him. It's hard to deny the fact that every act of lust is a failing, a falling away from Reality; therefore, a man *always* feels inferior to the woman after he has used her.

Most men cannot tolerate the fact that normal women have very little sex drive. A man's ego is threatened when he sees that the woman doesn't share his lustfulness, because an ego that cannot use cannot survive. Not only does an innocent woman fail to support a man's ego; she deflates it. When the wind goes out of his sails, he feels that he either has to dry up and blow away, or ruin that woman's innocence by showing her how to "get with it." He naturally decides to seduce her, to get her *under* him as a prop for his ego. So it is that the greater guilt belongs to the man, but the woman's relative innocence combines with her actual power to threaten his ego again and again. To put it crudely, a sophisticated, well-dressed lady makes a man feel self-conscious, perhaps a little awkward, whereas a naughty, naked female fascinates him and converts his anxiety into the anticipation of pleasure.

The situation is the same today as it is said to have been in the beginning, when Adam used Eve to support his ambition to be God. When a most ungodly animal popped out of Adam, instead of the God they expected, Eve had no choice but to become a mere female herself in order to play the supporting role to her male animal. As long as man continues to descend from a point of perfection, the problems that accompany his descent will continue to multiply until he finally recognizes the imperfections inherent in the man/woman relationship, and resolves them through True Love.

You men, my male readers, must become aware of your origin, the source of your problems with women. You must see that the male sex drive is the physical evidence of pride's failing, and you must see that your wives are painfully aware of that fact, even though you are not. Sitting on your wobbly throne, you require your woman to worship you and serve your ego, as though you were some kind of god. If you don't see it now, the day will surely come when you will discover that the "king" is the court jester and the court jester is the "king." And what a vicious monarch she is!

You must eventually see that there is something wrong with looking to woman as the source of love. As a man, you are the one who should be the source of love for your wife, even as the God you should serve is the only possible source of your own power to love at all. It is only a matter of time before you discover that your love for a woman has never been more than a need to sustain what is wrong with you—and that which is wrong with you is what is wrong with her. You have probably made sure of that.

Marriage can be a noble institution with a profound mystical significance. But husband and wife would be wise to watch for the telltale signs of lustful indulgence; and later on in life, they should be consciously prepared to phase out sex altogether. If marriage is the way you choose to go, the key to your immortality will lie in the way you practice sex in the early years, and the way you leave it behind after it has served its purpose.

Be advised that whenever your wife behaves in

some unreasonable way following a sexual relationship, you can take it as a sign that she is reacting to your lustful abuse of her. As time goes on, and you persist in wanting more sex than is reasonable—at least, from her point of view—she will use all kinds of unreasonable behavior in order to get back at you.

So then, as a young man, you may enjoy your wife and have a natural season of sexual expression without much suffering, until the day you begin to see what it is that you are expressing. It won't harm a man to practice sex, provided he remains conscious of the truth concerning it, which is: More sex does not a Heaven make; as a matter of fact, less sex is better. You should not use a wife for all she is worth, and think of it as love. It is not.

As a man, you should seek to join the woman to your own life pattern, to enlist her as your helpmate in working toward the goals that you intuitively know to be right for you. You must not be too eager to join yourself to her in complete sexual abandonment, lest you lose sight of your responsibilities along with your self-control. You may have discovered already that a woman derives great pleasure from the loving closeness of a man's body and does not want all the tender moments to end in earth-shaking climax. You would do well to learn how to extend and receive affection, with no end in view other than the savoring of it as an expression of the real love between you. Until you are able to forbear from spoiling every affectionate interlude with the completed sex act, you will never know how much true affection your wife actually feels toward you—she will be too afraid of "setting you off."

Through his climax, the man enters the woman and becomes the extension of the hell in her. Love—correcting love—can not be felt by the woman until the man becomes more moderate in his sexual use of her. The reason for this is that, on his way down from grace, man joined himself to the woman, and through the sin of pride, his ego has become sexually grounded in her. Contemporary man, born of woman, naturally seeks to complete the cycle of his earthly ego life with a female, but he should also discover what is inherently wrong with the relationship on the other side of the sexual experience. Indeed, it seems to be ordained that most men should fully experience female charms, so that eventually the hell side of sex can be revealed and the bubble of delusion burst. All ego striving must finally come to rest, because some day, as the climax of climaxes, the soul matures to realize the truth of its heritage.

You must bear in mind that man, through original sin, is committed to striving in earthy ways to survive and to renew his ego from the woman he has used and has come down to need. But he must be very careful not to add more pride of ambition to the work he must do, and the sex he must experience, lest he descend again and again. Because it is the fruit of the pride of ambition, sex, practiced unwisely, supports the pride that leads back to more failing and to still stranger sex drives.

By pridefully viewing sex as love, you turn sex into lust; and because lustful men crave worship for their failings, you have to see your failings as virtues. Since the beginning, all men have been committed to finding themselves through a woman, under the delusion that the completed "self" they are about to find will turn out to be none other than God. As each failing appears, it must be properly worshipped by the woman as a virtue and propitiated with sex offerings.

Through lust, a man can never complete his natural cycle and develop into the man he was meant to be. He can not possibly arrive at the threshold of Reality, because he has lost the ground, the humility, that allows the Light of God to restore his descended identity to its former bright state of grace. Such men see Reality as a threat, a source of unwelcome conflict.

Lust usually arises through a superstubborn, ambitious state of consciousness. Ambitious men are very active sexually, because ambition *always* results in spiritual failing, attended by physical compensations. Ambitious men, being wrong men, need reassurance; so they use sex in two ways: first, to command worship, and then, to stoke the proud ambition that will lead inevitably back to the need for more sexual reassurance.

It is this cycle of sexual reinforcement of pride that causes a man to continue in the falling direction, and that calls up the evil in the female to rise to the occasion of his failing. Thus, the man's need, masquerading as love, is what gradually changes the woman into a frustrated witch. If she is sensitive to what is going on inside her, her resentment can drive her into fits of depression. She has to be aware that people always sustain their pride and justify their wrongs by electing someone they see as more wrong to serve them. Tyranny always comes disguised as a lover, and requires the "loved" one to cooperate in its own ruination.

The True Love I have referred to in the previous pages can enter only through one kind of relationship.

And outside of the marital union, it cannot exist at all. A man who joins himself to a woman outside of wedlock can never be anything but a slave of the hell in woman, no matter how loyal he thinks he is in his commitment to her. Sex outside marriage is motivated by nothing but sexual use, and it cuts you off from the possibility of finding the divine love potential that exists in the honest man/woman relationship. The man who seeks to preserve a little freedom for himself by using a woman outside of marriage actually joins himself to the woman, and enters a no-holds-barred world of chaos, where he lives as the extension of her private hell until it kills them both.

There are laws governing the soul, or the psyche. When we fail to obey those laws, we change our reference point, and the change in reference point changes us. Inasmuch as those laws have been preserved by those who loved them and lived by them, we are aware of their existence, but they no longer seem to pertain to us. They may be enshrined in the laws of the land, and we may obey them out of sheer self-interest, but our heart is not in the observance. We have stepped outside of their protective boundary. And, once we have taken that step, we have alienated ourselves from that which can mold our nature from within. Obviously, if there were no such laws governing the world of Reality, we would be free to take our pleasure where we see it, and flit from flower to flower like a butterfly. We would not even need a government at all. Can you imagine what our world would be like if we all decided at once to kick over the traces and "do our own thing"? Fortunately, most of us don't have to try it in order to know that we could never get away with it.

If you are troubled, it is because your ego has crossed over the threshold of divine law, and is struggling to find the godly freedom it feels entitled to know. You have transgressed and forgotten the moral law that could have sustained your faith, and you have been forced to rationalize everything you have done. You have mindlessly sought comfort from the misleading spirit that tempted you to do wrong. Fortunately, there is a way back.

If you take hold of what is right in your heart, you will see Reality only in what is Real, and you will cease to respond to anything else. You will know Truth, and it will be your only guide. But if you fail, if you do respond to evil, you will find it difficult to stop responding. The sexual response of the male is the embodiment of this principle. As long as his ego remains prideful, he looks on his mortal wound as a glorious way to death.

Once you have crossed the mystic border of your psyche, or soul, you deliver yourself over to whatever enticed you to defect to its force field, and you are now powerless to resist the pressures it can exert. So you sin again and again. In the area of sexuality, you seek comfort from the woman for what she has made of you, and by making excuses, you bar the way to the Light that could redeem you and restore you to your former dignity and self-control. So you slide deeper into sin and break more of those unspoken rules. As you change and become more corrupt, you receive into yourself the nature and identity of your beguiler. In time, you are invaded, not only by the woman herself, but by her guiding spirit also.

Coming back to the subject of marriage, I hope you realize that I'm not asking you to take the vow of chastity. Few of us are ready to go that far, and the fact that there are so many bad marriages does not mean that marriage itself is bad. God gives us marriage as the answer to our earthy, ego-animal needs. He has ordained Holy Matrimony to be the medium through which the mortal sexual man and woman can one day go beyond sex to the realization of Him in perfect harmony. Everything serves God's purpose. In marriage, the inherited failing, sex, produces children who may also find His salvation. And children and wives stress men for the love they seek and have yet to know.

When a man becomes a father, he is compelled to reach deep inside himself for the wisdom not found in books. He must have a lot more going for him than what it took to make children. He needs the Love that transcends his need for the woman's body; without it, he cannot grow to be a good father and a good husband.

The very act of reaching within himself for answers to the problems of fatherhood sets the stage for grace to enter a man's life. No man can practice shameless lust with his wife and retain the authority that can inspire honest respect from his children; one lifestyle must give way to another. Children are perceptive beings; they sense any control the woman might have over the man. In a wordless way, they detect where their father stands with their mother, and they respond to him accordingly: with contempt or respect. Responding with contempt, children develop their mother's power over their father, because they *are* their mother's children, viewing him through her eyes, as a donkey, an object of use.

The head of the ideal family is the father, not the mother. As God is the head of Christ, Christ is the head of man, man the head of woman, and woman the head of the children. When that spiritual chain of command breaks down, chaos rules the roost in the form of the unloved, uncorrected spirit of the mother. Even when she does not rule directly, she rules indirectly. Whenever you see a violent, dominating father, you are looking at a man who does not know how to deal with the woman or the children. Because he has failed them, they gang up on him and torment him until he can no longer resist the temptation to overcome them with violence. Very often, the guilt he feels as the result of his violent behavior may cause him to become weak, docile, and passive. So, either way, through violence or passivity, he abnegates his authority and hell passes from the mother to the children, to perpetuate itself from generation to generation.

What a woman wants, whether she realizes it or not, is to be conquered by Love. But how can real love exist in a home that reeks with the stale death smell of sexuality? Where two persons tolerate each other for their respective advantage: men for sex, women for security?

The spark of Love shines most brightly in those moments when a man stands up to his wife, or for that matter, to anyone, to proclaim his allegiance to what is right. Life offers us the possibility of enlivening many such delicate moments, and no one can afford to let a single one of them pass unheeded, no matter what he stands to lose personally. Of course, some of those moments require no action at all; patience alone will often speak more eloquently than words. The point is that we must never seek peace at any price by leaving error unchallenged by word, deed, or patient silence. We must stay aware lest we give courage to the evil that is trying to overtake the people all around us, the people who need the love that can come only through our obedience to principle. To fail is to wither away, to die. True Love comes through little moments well met, for it is only in those moments that your fellow being can see and feel where you are coming from. In each test, people see what you are like inside and will respond in accordance with what *they* are like inside. Don't be upset if the brush with truth strikes terror in them and they drop you like a hot potato. Later on, in another situation, your words or the loving expression on your face can come back to them with new meaning and they will share your world in spirit. As a matter of fact, we must guard against the temptation to take so much pride in our "ability to correct" that we find ourselves offering correction to those who are more innocent and closer to Truth than we are. Correction is nothing we can "lay" on another, but something that comes about when its presence in ourselves shines so brightly that it lights the way for others.

Every soul contains a little bit of the script of heaven or hell, and we who are heaven-centered can tell what part others are playing by the way they read their lines. Even though we may not know what the script is about on an intellectual level, we can tell intuitively whether or not a person is being gracious with us. We watch for timing. We know when they fumble their lines and assume the role of tempter/villain, as opposed to hero/lover. We know, yet we cannot say to them, "you should have been more considerate." It is not our place to tell people when and where to be gracious. We cannot always speak up openly about such subtle matters, but by staying on center, we do come to understand what people are about; we can see when there is no love there, only selfishness. And selfishness tempts; it does not love. But as long as we are not tempted, we are protected.

Love can never come through a man's submission to his wife, to his becoming her little puppy dog. Nor can love prevail when a man grinds the woman into the ground with violence in an effort to force her respect, or when he tries to buy her respect with material treats. Love can come into the home only when a man has the power and grace to enlist his wife's cooperation in obedience to principle. If she has been schooled in the wily ways of the temptress, he must be as stubborn in his correctness as she is in her willfulness, as wise as she is crafty, and as calm as she is confusing. In time, when he has withstood the fury of the test, he will win his soul and live happily ever after with the woman he has loved truly.

Speak boldly, then, without self-righteousness or malice, and the words will become arrows from Cupid's bow, piercing the heart of your beloved and freeing her from the service of error. But if you soften your comments through weakness, fear of losing her favors by hurting her feelings, your need for correction will be as great as hers. Whether you speak boldly, or pussyfoot around, if you are trying to correct the obvious flaws in your wife while hanging on to your own, you will merely give her the right to judge you back. She will be much too busy with your wrong to see her own, and you will give the enemy within her the power to go on tormenting you. Remember that only correctness can correct.

A word of rebuke, guilelessly spoken, flies straight to the target. The recipient's first reaction may be to recoil with resentment or to flare up with violence. But if the message in the missile rings true, in that it is completely non-judgmental, its very purity will cause the person being rebuked to feel the carpet being pulled out from under his resentment, and shame will lead to correction.

Once you learn not to react to wrong with emotion, you will be able to look objectively at the wrong itself, and beyond the wrong, to the cause. If you do this with your sexual drives, you will come to see the origin of your ego's failing that is encoded in your mind and body. You will see that the image of the woman in your mind has something to do with its having gotten there through an original failing or sin. And, as a man, you will see how your ego clings to that image in order to escape the shame of what sin has done to you.

When you are ready, if you will learn to let the pain—the need for sexual relief or self-expression—pass, you will then see how you "leak" energy to the woman as the price for her support. This is the life force, exuding from the man's reaching toward the woman, that excites the female nature when men fail to love honestly. And once the woman falls and becomes dependent on that vital force, she will excite the man for it, and tease and nag him for it, until the day he dies.

Now, men also get some energy through sex. The sex act energizes a man's ego to make him ambitious, thus priming him to fail, and most of the power goes to the woman. Men do not see this draining effect, because their minds are so lost in the pleasure of the moment that they fail to see themselves being drained, and they don't understand the strange behavior patterns of their wives, who feel obliged to take liberties with them. It is this male ego weakness that seduces a woman out of her center, and causes her to exist on keeping him out of his center, thus causing him to "live" off of his dying to her.

What a man must learn to do, then, is to lie with his wife in innocent togetherness from time to time to discover the subtle joy of extending the spiritual love that follows his saying "no" to lust and letting it pass. Believe it or not, there is good pleasure in this discipline. In time, he will be able to see the leaking effect that comes from body contact alone. It will eventually diminish as the result of being observed, and Love will gush into the relationship. Light will suffuse the home, and you will be blessed in everything you do.

12 How to Have a Perfect Marriage

If a woman fails to find in her husband the father she never knew as a child, the man will surely bring out in his wife the mother he has known all his life.

A young woman leaves her parents to complete a natural as well as a spiritual cycle. She yields her body in marriage to the man she believes capable of fulfilling her with a love that is more meaningful and pure than any she has ever known. She expects the natural, physical fulfillment to be transcended shortly by another higher form of love, the kind her father never could give her. Because he could not, she has to pin her hopes on finding that love in marriage. She will often marry an older man, because it is her father whose mysterious male presence has overshadowed her life. Whether her expectations of true love have been met, or cruelly dashed to the ground, it is to her father, or to her idealization of what a father should be, that she has always looked for protective strength. It follows that, in the ideal marriage, the day comes when her husband becomes her father, and she becomes his offspring in spirit.

To find the perfect marriage, every woman must look beyond masculinity to the inner man, and she must find the one whose love for what is right in principle is greater than his desire for her. If she is lucky enough to find such a man, she can safely join herself to him, but if she settles for a weak man, he will join himself to her, and she will find herself in the driver's seat, which is often the last place she wants to be. She will have to say goodbye to her dreams of a strong man to protect her.

Getting back to the ideal situation, the father identity in a principled man is capable of separating the woman from any "female" wiles she might have adopted in order to catch him. Once she is assured of his integrity, once she knows that he will always "be there" for her, she can throw the game playing out the window, settle down, and be herself. A weak man, on the other hand, will call out to her for every ploy, every stratagem she can possibly develop, in order to hang onto a shaky security. She will have to become a witch to support his ego-centered lifestyle.

A woman soon discovers which type of man she has joined herself to, primarily through the sex experience. The way a husband relates to his wife in bed tells her all she has to know about him. She soon discovers whether he is feeding her with love, or feeding *on* her with lust. A fatherly man has a genuine concern for the woman's real need, and that concern overrides his own physical need for sex. He can say "no," both to his own need and to any unwarranted demand on his wife's part; so he does not walk on eggshells to hang onto her favor, nor does he spoil her.

A woman soon learns the meaning of "frustration" when she discovers that she is being used to satisfy a

man's vanity. As she nears the end of her baby-pro-
ducing cycle of life, especially, she resents her husband's continuing use of her to gratify himself. She
feels threatened by sex when her husband fails to give
her the special love from the dimension beyond sex
that would have the power to free her from the female
role. The more he wallows in sex, the more she wallows in frustration and resentment. Unfortunately, as
long as a female reacts with rage and resentment, the
male does not see what is wrong with him and his
needs; so he will tend to reply to her tantrums with sex
love. And she will reply to his sex love with a secret
loathing that will render her so guilty that she will have
to continue relieving her guilt in a sexual way.

Female surrender is nearly always a form of conquest. The mere fact that a woman is a woman is all
the stress a failing man needs to excite him sexually,
and a man is never at his strongest and best when his
tongue is hanging out. Unfortunately, it is a situation in
which he finds himself a great deal of the time. Any
pressure that is severe enough to cause him to "cop
out" will excite him sexually in respect to his tormentor,
even if it happens to be his own child or another man.
From that point on, even though he might not go so far
as to call it "love," his sexual reactions will color and
enhance his emotional reactions toward his pressure
sources. He will dream of his tormentors the way he
dreams of women. He will also get an unwholesome
"charge" out of barroom brawls and contact sports.

In the same way that parents often try to overcome a
child's tantrums by giving in, a man will give in to the
pressure of a female tease. The evidence of his failing is

the sexual desire, the ravaging kind of "love" that prompts and reinforces a dictatorial response in the female. She is more aware of the dynamics of their fall than he is, and regrets having caught the tiger by the tail. She would love to turn back the clock and return to innocence; she cries out for love in vain. The only answer he knows how to give her is more sex, more power for her madness.

Fortunately, there comes a time when the natural season for sex has run its course, and you will know that time has come when sexual desires begin to cause anxiety. At that point, a man should begin to see the folly of pouring all his life force into them, and he should start to draw back.

A woman's secret resentment has a terrible power all its own. It can cause a man to feel so thoroughly rejected that he becomes impotent, or he can resent back and blow the smoldering coals of resentment into a raging inferno of violence. A woman can use the resentment-filled silences to conjure up tidbits for her ego to munch on; but the trouble with this manipulation is that she is never really happy with the results. If she has been using resentment to keep her husband away, she begins to feel lonely for the human presence—even his. She also feels guilty for harboring such an unloving attitude, and without sexual love to comfort her, she will begin to look back on the past guilts that she has been repressing. So there she goes again. She gives in sexually, only to become resentful and sick to her stomach all over again.

When a woman uses resentment to keep her husband from importuning her for sex, she swells up with judgment, and even though she might develop a secret need for sexual "love," she is afraid of what it has always done to her. So she unconsciously solves the problem of guilt that has resulted from her judgment and dishonesty by stepping up her resentment to such a pitch that it drives her husband to impotency. Now she has the perfect justification for her resentment. She can now imagine herself, and represent herself to others, as being a normal, love-hungry woman whose husband can't take care of her. Her resentment not only makes her guilty; it prepares her to try to make up for the guilt by way of the sex trip. She may even become so demanding that she frightens the man away entirely, and she can glory secretly in her judgment of his neglect.

Frequently, the stalemate I have just described results in a completely distorted view of the relationship, especially on the part of friends and relatives who are not close enough to it to sense the dynamics involved in it. To the innocent eye, it will appear as though the couple has managed to transcend sex entirely, thanks to the great love they have borne each other. Nothing could be farther from the truth. Behind the perfect picture of triumphant resolution, the couple squirms in the frustrating ambivalence of lusting and loathing at the same time.

After years of simmering in such a strained relationship, either the husband or the wife is likely to boil over suddenly and take up with somebody else—perhaps, with a total stranger. Eventually, one of them will no longer put up with the playacting in public, or the other's sullen resentment in private, and will dare to seek relief in someone else's arms. Of course, it will be the same old journey, and it will end in the same old frustration as long as it is based on the same old illusions.

Sexual experimentation within the framework of marriage is perfectly natural and moral up to a point, but the time comes when we should go on to better things. The woman's plight is especially grievous, inasmuch as she is so often held to an earthy role by a selfish man's need for her support. While it is entirely possible for any of us, man or woman, to find salvation on our own, a woman brought up on traditional values tends to look to her husband to lead the way to their spiritual growth. When he fails to do so, she feels trapped.

While a woman will often use surrender for the sole purpose of conquering a man, she is also capable of surrendering her will to a man out of genuine respect for him and his values. Similarly, a young son can obey his mother out of fear of what she might do to him if he doesn't or simply because he respects her wishes and is pleased to acknowledge her authority in the home. The kind of world that develops in the microsphere of the home depends entirely on the character of the governing authority. It is almost impossible to respect what is not respectable, so it is an exercise in futility to require anyone to do so. When a disreputable drunk of a father insists on getting the respect due him as the head of the house, he naturally doesn't get it. All he gets is more gross and more demanding, even though his victims might reward him with a sullen capitulation out of fear and to relieve their guilt. When the victim is pushed too far, he revolts. A wife overflows with revulsion and takes it out on the children. A son rebels against his willful mother; if he manages to get the upper hand, he becomes violent, and if he fails, he becomes effeminate.

The moral of the story is simply that we cannot respect, nor can we expect others to respect, what is not inherently respectable. To be forced into conformity by ungodly pressure is to be forced to live a lie. In the end, Reality must be served, for God is not mocked. You can expect to receive only the respect that is due you in acknowledgment of your gracious obedience to the authority above you. It follows that the ultimate authority in any home must be the God who created us. If you are beginning to feel like Rodney Dangerfield because you aren't getting any respect, you would do well to take a good look at your right to deserve it.

A God-serving man is the natural authority in the home. Only such a man can override any residual female guile in his wife's nature and overshadow her influence on the children. When the man abnegates his authority in return for his wife's sexual favors, it is the spoiled, guileful nature of the female that rules the roost and ruins the children. The male child grows up to be insecure and unmanly, and he will often seek his male identity in a homosexual relationship. Or he will seek the ground of his being in a wife, who will be to him what his mother has been to his father. And the girl child will leave home to seek in some weak man the kind of father she has never known. The absence of a strong father figure in the home makes growing up difficult, if not actually hazardous, for all concerned.

A man's lusty nature with its female-inspired sexual

demand is a form of authority to the average woman; and for a season, she may surrender to this natural need. But she must do so in a way that does not flatter and promote his ego—or her own, by devious means.

Remember that surrender is one of the roundabout ways of gaining ascendancy over another person. You simply agree to serve the dominant personality in such a way that, as his victim, you have elected him lord; in other words, you are the boss-maker and he is just the boss, dependent on your queenly approval. Of course, the win-by-losing technique does not always work on a hard-shelled, dyed-in-the-wool autocrat, who has been brought up to expect and to get the last drop of blood from the hoi polloi under him. He just gets louder and viler in his demands, and his wife becomes more fearful and submissive, trying unconsciously to set a good example and manipulate him with her "loving service" to be "good" like other men.

After the sexual phase of life has been fully experienced, comes the pain—the pain of having to reckon with the spiritual side of life that has been largely ignored in the heat of passion. As I have already pointed out, man has two origins, two births—one, physical, and the other, spiritual. When he nears the end of the physical phase, he must be born again in the spirit. That is to say, he must lay aside his ego/female foundation. Rather than command his wife to be his source of love, he must start to reject any moves she might make in that direction; for now it is his turn to be the source and giver of love to his wife. Careful! Not the kind love that gives to get back, but the kind of love for love's sake that is patient, objective, and totally unconcerned with the concepts of losing or gaining for one's self.

In their sexual union, the woman sustains the prideful, death-oriented ego of her man; and at first, her doing so has a value, insofar as it contributes to making them both aware that there is something wrong with it. It is one of the first steps of the physically mature male and female on their way to becoming man and wife. The man's ego need, fulfilled, brings the female to motherhood and responsibility, and him to fatherhood. At this point, he discovers the awful truth; he is just one of the kids!

A one-dimensional relationship suffices for the making of babies, but to be a real parent, man needs the authority from the other dimension of love. Children need, and sometimes even crave, correction. They need to be rescued from their natural ego-selfish state. In their formative years, the love they receive from their mothers is sensual and instinctual. Her body warmth and ego support help the infant's ego to grow into the mature child of nature. But children are as dual in nature as the rest of us. They need the same two kinds of love: earthly love from mother, and heavenly love from father.

But how can father give the child the corrective love he needs, as long as father is competing with the child for mother's support of his own childish and sensual ego needs? He cannot. So the woman finds herself supporting two children, her baby and her husband. She discovers that she has somehow replaced her husband as the authority in the home. Not only that, she is becoming a mother to the husband, who is becoming less of a man in the process. Just as Eve did in the Garden under the serpent's influence, she is causing her Adam to fall by sustaining him sexually in his natural state. Sooner or later, husband and wife will come face-to-face with the Adam-and-Eve syndrome; that is, they will if they don't misinterpret the lesson of their suffering.

A woman may eventually come to realize the truth about man and woman by yielding to her man and experiencing him just the way he is. As she matures, as she approaches the crossroad with her mate, she feels a kind of anxiety. Will they opt to somehow rise above their mortality, or will they descend into death through some "witchcraft" that seems to be impelling her against her will and beyond her ability to understand? At that point, she begins to fear and distrust all that she has been naturally enjoying, needing, and encouraging. And it is at that point that she sees her lover as the unprincipled child of her own private Hell, whose love amounts to nothing but a selfish need for ego support, without regard to what it might be doing to her.

Just as a child, or an egocentric man, needs mothering, so does a woman need fathering to help her overcome the problems of being a female. But what happens if she never finds a man with the potential to become a loving, respectable father? If all she can find is a one-dimensional, weak, vain male, looking for a "mama" to make him feel secure?

In the beginning, woman was man's child, cloned from his bones, and was called "woman" for that very reason. If she was intended to experience the continued cooperation and support of a man on her earthly sojourn, she will need the warmth of a man's body and soul. She will require his fatherly love to draw the woman out of the earth-born female. But in his pride and ignorance, a man will seldom allow such a development to occur. Because of his desperate need to be sustained in his life of pride, man turns the tables and draws on the woman's warmth rather than offer his own. Now, thanks to her sustaining it, the male emerges from the man, and the beast from the male. And who can respect the beast, other than the strange woman, looking for escape and adventure, who has not yet added her insanity to his.

The ability of a man to lie with his wife without violating her is a learned skill, not a natural instinct. If he can rise to such a remarkable challenge, it can only be by virtue of the Spirit of God abiding in him and making him aware of his wife's need for his selfless love. Originally, man was the father of woman, but when his failure to love brought out his animal nature, he became the woman's husband, as opposed to "taking her to wife."

There must come a time in the life of a potentially God-centered man when he must realize that he has feasted long enough on the pleasures of the world, and he must seek an answer to the question that is beginning to nag him: Is this all there is? One of the first things he is likely to see is that he has abnegated his responsibility toward his wife and family by putting his own ego satisfactions and ambitions first. Somehow, he must do what he can to crawl out from under the shadow of dependency on his wife, and free her from the dark cloud of his old needs, in such a way that they can travel the rest of the way by the Light of Reality.

The man who can let the moment of passion pass in

order that his wife might experience the love that can deny its own need is well on his way to restoring a godly order to the home. If you can rise to this challenge, your wife will see and feel that love, and she will respond in kind, with a new love and respect for you. She will gladly restore to you the leadership she may never have wanted in the first place; and you will become the authority your children have always needed. Both your wife and your children will know the correcting love that comes from the other dimension through self-denial. Under the leadership of principle, or real love, the Kingdom of Heaven expresses itself on earth. Your family will trust you implicitly, without questioning your motives, whereas before, no one ever believed you, even when you were not "guilty."

True Love is the step just beyond the compassion that led a man to start giving up sex. He will experience moments of failure and moments of triumph, but he will make no attempt to rationalize his failures into something more worthy. The woman who respects that man will not hate him for failing, because she loves the spirit that moves him, and she realizes that he is striving with himself for her sake. His sacrifice is an expression of Love. It is also an expression of real manhood in the making.

Of course, these things I have been saying will be meaningful revelations only to those who are searching for God's salvation, to the man and wife with the same searching attitude. The ideal couple, in other words. No Truth makes sense to the others.

13 No One Has To Die

A reading from the Book of Wisdom

It was the devil's envy that brought death into the world.

God did not make death,
nor does He rejoice in the destruction of the living.
For He fashioned all things that they might have being;
and the creatures of the world are wholesome.
And there is not a destructive drug among them
nor any domain of the netherworld on earth,
For justice is undying.
For God formed man to be imperishable;
the image of his own nature he made him.
But by the envy of the devil, death entered the world,
and they who are in his possession experience it.

—Wisdom 1:13-15; 2:23-24

God help us all if the anthropologists succeed in persuading us that we have evolved from apes, whose still more distant ancestors crawled out of the primordial slime. Such a belief, universally held, would set fire to our violent lower nature, and release us to rape, steal, and kill one another. If we really believed such a god-less idea, all the way down to the soles of our feet, we would disband the police force (something our gangs are trying very hard to do right now), open the jails, and burn the law books. We would feel that we had finally found the truth to set us ape-men free. We could throw away the old theology and law. We would be free to express our strictly-animal natures, to let down our hair, and be our rotten selves at last.

If we were to allow this satanic argument to govern us, we would know world chaos. It would free us from the control of laws that are already being strained to the limit by the miscreants among us. We would begin to reason: What is the point of laws that do nothing but rob us of the right to express our true nature? From a strictly scientific and humanistic point of view, man-made laws only hamper the free expression of natural law and stifle the evolutionary growth process. There are those who would argue that such laws can not possibly serve society, that they militate against social progress, and that our biggest social problem consists of having to handle society's natural refusal to abide by such "unnatural" restraints. But, freed from their restraints, could we really expect to evolve into a race of superbeings through the evolutionary process?

Let's look ahead a little. Can your ego bear to think about the super-brainy, large-craniumed creatures that might evolve from your seed many generations into the future? Can you visualize them looking back on us affectionately, or perhaps contemptuously, in the way that we look back on the great apes that are reputed to be our own ancestors? Can't you just see them purring contentedly, as they look back on you and gloat over how far they have surpassed you in every way? We should live so long!

The fact remains that we are the only creatures on earth who need laws and restraints; and that fact is proof enough that we are different and that there is something wrong with that difference. But it is not the law that is wrong. It is ourselves, for needing law.

Simple logic prevents us sensible folk from believing in the up-from-the-slime theory. Even if all our noses were rubbed in so-called scientific proof, such a belief would go against the grain of our common sense. By the same token, all dyed-in-the-wool, proud evolutionists are equally zealous in support of their brand of truth and are unable to stomach honest-to-goodness Truth.

If the evolution of man is the "truth" proud men are seeking, then anthropologists must be the high priests of scientific prejudice, dedicated to reading false meanings into every new "find" they unearth for their followers. Fortunately, some of us have been around long enough to know that the "experts" are constantly disagreeing with one another. And often, while today's expert is busy debunking yesterday's expert, another expert will proclaim that the day-before-yesterday's expert was on the right track after all! So much for scientific facts.

Those who go gung-ho for the evolutionary origin of man usually deny the existence of God as the Absolute Truth. But when they expunge higher realization from their consciousness, how in the world do they manage to see man as beholden only to some natural origin and order? Are they not trying to substitute one "absolute" (which they claim does not exist) for another? Just look at the absurd contradiction and the monumental ego behind the statement: "There is no Absolute Truth."

People of ancient times believed that the earth was the center of the universe. Before we dismiss this belief as laughable by today's knowledge and chalk it up to vanity, let us remember that in a very real sense, our ancestors were closer to Reality than we are today. While our science has shown us that the earth revolves around the sun, and the sun revolves around some other celestial object, we should not dismiss our ancestors' view, inasmuch as the two views are taken from different perspectives, and both are correct.

If enlightened men of old were informed of today's scientific truth, as I am sure they were, they would attest to the correctness of both concepts. The reason is that if you view the universe from a strictly scientific viewpoint, with metaphysical vision totally suspended, all you will be able to see is the earth revolving around the sun. But if you view man as he could be, see him by the Light that can make him over into what he can really be, you will see him standing at the center of the Universe, with all that is relative to him revolving around him. Through believing in, and being At One with his Creator, the Christ-centered man stands at the beginning, the hub of all creation, providing an ultimate frame of reference for all that is. Thus, a man who can realize his proximity to the center of the universe can also realize the truth of the scientific viewpoint, the only one that is possible for the carnal, spiritually blind, earthy mind.

Although they insist that all is relative, and there is no such thing as an "absolute," vain, blind evolutionists insist on clinging to their own absolute belief in the evolutionist theory of man. Is it not strange that learned scientists, schooled in logic, can contradict themselves without even knowing they are doing it? But when we look at them from our viewpoint, of course, we see how their limited scientific vision blinds them to their own contradictions. They simply can not perceive their own wrongs, because they lack the vision to see anything clearly.

A Divine Paradox cannot contradict itself. Without an Ultimate Divine factor, knowledge often does contradict itself, and men can not see that it does. Let me point out here that a vain man who prides himself on his "spirituality" can also see himself as the center of the universe, but he is incapable of grasping the scientific fact because his ego is threatened by facts.

Our paradox then—the scientific observation from a metaphysical viewpoint—does not contradict itself as long as we are related to, and realize by, the highest viewpoint. We see both truths, one by the Light of the other. Only a special kind of person, one who is capable of loving God and therefore realizing Truth, can see both truths, the scientific truth that is superseded by the metaphysical Truth, an end by the Light of the beginning.

Now, then, it should be easy for you seekers to see why the shortsighted, rote-educated humanoids want to peg their origin in the evolutionary slime. If they were correct, we would be looking at an orderly evolution toward the ultimate perfection of our race. But is that what you see? Of course, all vain people see every change in their culture as a sign of progress; but seeing men see most scientific achievements as compensations for spiritual failing, unworthy of being taken seriously as signs of human progress. Evolving creatures, under natural law, have no need for inventions, nor do they need civilizing, because they evolve in accordance with the order that has been programmed into them.

Let us look at man's origin from a more enlightened point of view, one that observes the evolutionary process as having been triggered by a falling away from a higher order of existence. If that is the case, we might expect a devolutionary process to claim us, a sort of "devolving" evolution of earthy compensations, accompanied by inner and outer conflict. The only way we would know how to treat one another would be as animals, rather than as people. As a result, we would come to need some kind of order, and it would have to be imposed on us from the outside. In other words, we would come to need the kind of law (religion, really) that we left behind when we fell from the Inner Ground of Reality.

All enlightened men know that there are two truths that can set us free. One "truth" makes a monkey out of man by setting out to prove that the monkey self is the original man, and is therefore pure and innocent as it comes into the world. But that philosophy, carried to its conclusion, tends to lead ape men chaotically above the hedge of law and restraint. Satan's goal is to destroy mankind; first, by taking him away from God, and then, away from the moral laws he needs until he finds God's salvation from the law.

When it is properly realized, the seeking man's Truth

actually saves him from the prison of creaturehood; it also raises him above the need for governance that is required by a free-falling nature. After such a man has fallen from the modifying influence of Reality, it is only a matter of time before he wakes up feeling self-conscious and guilty, and he sees death staring him in the face. He sees what he has become, but the disobedient ego that caused him to fall will seek to blind him to the nature of Reality, his original state of innocence. Pride, instigator of the fall, the snake in the grass of the subconscious, never wants the host soul to see its own error; it would have us see Truth as the enemy, and the seducer as the friend.

Why should we bother to challenge Pride, one of the sacred cows of our society? Why should we seek to know the truth of our lost identity? What purpose can the knowledge serve?

The answer is clear. We are creatures of belief. It is through wrong belief that we become wrong. And we take pride in our wrong until some stray shaft of light strikes a dark corner of our consciousness, and we wake to our guilt. This is the moment of Truth. The choice is clear. We must either shore up our faith in the rightness of our wrong belief, or seek the original ground of our being and seek to obey it in spirit and in deed.

Because the seeking mind appreciates both spiritual and mundane truths, one by the light of the other, we do see why the earth-minded man sees only his evolutionary source. We are all failing, seeking to find redemption from guilt; the honest man seeks in one way, the proud ape-man in another. But we are all seeking, and that fact alone is evidence that we are lost.

In an uncomplimentary sense, evolution would have you exist as a mere link in an endless chain, with bigger and more glorious apes yet to rise from the seed of your seed of your seed, *ad infinitum.* In this context, the best life you can hope for here is to live again, and a little better, through them, as expressed by the aphorism: "Your children are your future." But if we shall one day be they, who are we now? We can have no special human identity as the "image and likeness of God," for the spirit of ancient monkeys is perpetuating itself in us.

Animals obviously have no need for our truths or laws. If we differ from the others only insofar as we can think and use tools, then we have no need to seek the truth of anything, least of all our origin, for we remain rooted in that origin. But are we?

The answer is simple. Man differs from the lower animals, not in terms of compensating, rule making, tool making, or in any way you can think of, other than or aside from, his possession of consciousness. We alone have a consciousness that is capable of choosing between right and wrong, or realizing God, Truth, and the Absolute—or of going the other way and denying God in order to preempt His power for ourselves. The Pride that denies the existence and power of God separates us from Truth. We will be charged and found guilty until we succeed in finding the perfect Truth, or the perfect excuse.

Animals cannot stray from their predestined course because they have no consciousness, and therefore, no power to conceptualize a non-instinctive, creative way to go, much less choose to go that way. But the consciousness of man endows him with the power to believe and to choose, to accept or deny the prompting of his conscience, and to change his destiny as the result of his choice.

Man was created to know and to obey his Creator. When he rejects God, man tries hard to believe that his fallen self is infallible. He is too proud to admit that he has made wrong choices, too pride-ridden to face the reality of his failing. He moves pridefully onward to ever greater folly, rarely seeing it as folly, preferring to call it a problem or a challenge. He sees his animalistic compensations as growth, and the excretions of his pride as progress and civilization. Be not beguiled by the boasts of culture, or confuse culture with civilization, the outward and sincere expression of reverence for an overriding principle.

Let us take a look at the "undeniable" fact of death by the light of what I have just been saying about evolution. Remember that death entered the world in answer to the proud challenge of an ego that would be God, and an ego that proud does not back down easily. How could it admit to the possibility of having made a wrong choice? Such an ego, seeing change and deterioration and death in the world around him, must ascribe what he sees to the inevitable working out of natural law, over which he naturally cannot be expected to have any control. And if he can't control it, he need look no more deeply into it. He must accept the inevitability of death, just as he must rummage around in old caves to dig up old bones and fossils that will support his materialistic belief in evolution and natural (hence, believable) law.

What the ego fails to see is that death came into existence through the attitude of pride that still has him in a stranglehold and still causes him to see death as inevitable and undeniable. Death, in the light of the Highest Reality, is the proof and the punishment for our disobedience. But how can a proud ego see by the light of Reality? The stubborn, faithless sinner must accept death as his inheritance, as all he has to look forward to and believe in (along with taxes, of course), and as the ultimate rest for his weary head. As he gets older, uglier, and farther from Reality, *his* only reality, Death, seems to beckon him with open arms. The god-*making*, as opposed to the God-*centered*, life is a debilitating life, and it ends as it must, in death.

Although some of us are able to observe death intuitively from two different perspectives, the egomaniac can see it only as a realistic, scientific, ineluctable *fact of life*. Of course, death is observable and it is real, but it originated, and still grows from, the very nature of pride, which, by denying Reality, fixates compulsively to the death state, the state in which it is unconsciously living. The nature of pride, creator of death, is oblivious to the sin of pride, and is therefore forced to see, and to accept as right and necessary, all the faults that it creates as a bulwark against Reality. Death, the logical end of a misspent life, pride's crowning creation, thus becomes the most unshakable belief of the proud ego.

The vain soul tries hard to make death and dying bearable, even noble, in ways too numerous to list. The way most commonly stressed, and already mentioned here, is to see death as a "rest," a reward at the end of life's struggle, a doorway to heaven.

When we were children, closer to Reality, we sensed that there was something wrong about death; but because we were unable to figure it out, or do anything to stop it, we simply tried to avoid thinking about it at all. By doing so, we were able to preserve our ego existence and false security concerning immortality. Unfortunately, when our values are centered on the preservation of our ego existence, to the exclusion of our spiritual identity, we must eventually come up against Death with our ego-blunted senses and see it as the ultimate, earth-shattering, life-eating Reality. Its awful presence makes believers of us whether we like it or not; we must accept the truth of it.

All our lives, after all, we have felt impelled to look on our failings—such as animal emotion, lust, and greed—as virtues, so why should we exclude death, the final failing, from the ranks of the good and the true. Our belief in death also provides us with a handy philosophic basis for excusing our egocentric behavior. Why should we bother to restrain our appetites as long as we are going to die, anyway? The two-pack-a-day smoker often admits that he might be shortening his life, but "what the heck," he says, "I'll enjoy it more!" Of course, he is overlooking the fact that he might be spending his last few months hooked up to a tank of oxygen, and struggling for every breath.

Let us not forget that death came into existence through deception. But I'm not asking you to look on death as an illusion; death is real. It isn't the only product of deception—we all are. And, because we are creatures who depend on proofs and facts, we must believe in death. The original deception, operating through pride, has made it real for us.

Our lack of faith has made death real, and it has turned us into children of harsh realities. All prideful, death-justified, and female-motivated people have their lives neatly arranged around death. They would be terrified if you were to suggest to them that death need not be inevitable. You would ruin all their ego/mental calculations and excuses; you would pull the rug out from under them.

Remember, the egocentric views life in a single dimension, because he can not conceive of a Reality greater than himself. His pride forbids him to see death as the evidence of sin, which it surely *is*, so he must see it as a good thing. Any person who is carnal-minded, whose life revolves around women and death, is unconsciously forced to cling to a death-as-truth concept in order to justify his dying, earthy existence.

Let us look at the principle involved once more, from a slightly different angle. No vain ego can deny death as the ultimate truth until it finds the faith to resist the lie that created the morbid death reality in the first place. We are born devoid of original faith. We are doubt-lie-woman-death oriented, obliged to doubt Truth in order to accept death as part of life; and we will continue in the direction we are going as long as we reject the Higher Reality, Who says, "In Him death is made alive."

Remember the two truths in one: the death truth, which, when viewed by the Light of Reality, through the subtle prod of faith, is seen as death personified and is asked: O grave, where is your victory? O death, where is your sting?

If an extremely vain person were suddenly to be seized by the truth of immortality, it would only be because his vanity has persuaded him that he has become, or become one with, God—therefore, he can not die. His belief in eternal life, and his rejection of death, are not supported by real faith; they are simply denials of the self-evident, scientific fact of death. Such a sinner not only denies Reality; he also rejects what is for him a true scientific fact, and thus deceives himself again. Death will continue to be a morbid fact of life for him, whether he rejects it or accepts it. So be warned: don't waste your time on trying to believe in immortality by devious mental means. Be patient. The day may come when your searching will grace you to see it clearly, as a fact.

We are inherently ambitious and lie/death oriented, thanks to the same old need to be God that "killed" Adam. Most of us are still unable to view one truth (the scientific one) by the Light of the Other. We often see ourselves as gods, alone in the universe. We are full of excuses, alive in our imagination, dead in Reality.

Some of us are mad enough to see death as a neat way to sidestep God's judgment. They assume that when they die, all will be forgiven. Some of us are even silly enough to believe that everything will cease to exist when they die, so that, by doing so, they will take death away with them.

You may have a secret fear of discovering the Truth, because you think you will die if you do. And you are absolutely right. You will. That is, something within you will die, the part that you probably identify as "you," the vain, ambitious nature that can not live in the Light of Reality. It will die, and when it dies it will take with it the evil spirit of pride that has made a home in you.

Does not the anticipation of pride's death fill you with a godly joy? No? More likely, you are so identified with your tattered cloak of pride that its loss would not only leave you naked; it would kill you. If I speak Truth, and believe me, I do, I threaten your proud lifestyle. Listen to me at the risk of losing the smug sense of security you have derived from a death-justified life. Does the mere thought of immortality scare you "to death"?

Alas for you unbelievers who can not see the truth in anything unless you can dress yourself up in it and put on an act under its hypnotic influence. These words are not for those who flirt with words and place their hope in death. They are for you who have hope in life, you who are blessed to see clearly the Truth they seek to reveal. If you can receive their witness, these words can cause you to doubt the lie that has made you doubt the Truth. They will free you from any lingering belief in the lie. Do you not see how doubt has cut you off from life, and how your doubt-self, or what is left of it, shudders on hearing these words of life?

The belief in evolution and death opens the door to futility, hopelessness, and despair—no wonder so many of us see life as meaningless. Once we reject Reality, all we see ahead of us is a bottomless pit, and the only way we can bear to face the lie-based reality is, actually, to reject it, too, by getting high on soul food, ego food, booze, dope, or other mind-blowing excitements.

All the morbid truths we discover in moments of lucidity on our "journey to glory" have been made real for us by our own folly. But if we will view the truth of hopelessness by the Light of the other Truth, hope, we can see that it is only the *proud* way of life that is hopeless, not the way of life that we were intended to follow. In our stubbornness and vanity, we hang onto our own proud way, and its relative truths: futility and death. We identify with these truths, so that as futility draws us ever closer to death, we feel that we are fulfilling our true purpose by remaining loyal to our beliefs, steadfast—and therefore, innocent—to the bitter end.

When we are ambitious, we are totally preoccupied with thoughts and imaginings, our constant companions. It never occurs to us that these vainglorious thoughts are devious, serving nothing but Hell. For heaven's sake, do not confuse them with intuitive insights that come from above, such as those you are finding in the words written here. Stand guard against words and ideas that "butter" you up; seek rather to be "waked" up by the astringent, non-sentimental quality of real Love.

Many dangerous forces in every society seek to have us die to them. There is nothing apostles of Satan want more than to make monkeys out of us, so that they may become our redeemers, leaders, and lawgivers. At this very moment, the high priests of science are gathering "evidence" from the far reaches of the earth to convert and placate the anxious egos of their troops. For an atheist to accept the prejudiced "evidence" of the high priests of science is just as much an act of faith, and therefore, religious, as it is for a God-centered man to believe in the fall of man. *Anything* that is based on faith is religious by nature, simply because the salvation offered by faith is based on the belief in truth.

Proof inspires the hypnotic faith of the faithless: it saves them from realizing the Truth. But we who seek to understand the nature of our wrongs do so in the hope that we might be saved from the fate of beasts, the hell that awaits the bodies without souls. The vain, faithless, gullible man is compulsively subject to scientific proof. If he can't get it "on good authority," he will invent it for himself out of the bits and pieces of what he knows to be true. But, because he lacks the Ultimate Standard of comparison, he winds up believing in whatever promises the greatest benefit to the particular need of his foolish ego.

Any man of science can tell you that the proof of any scientific fact is impossible without a criterion on which to base it. But unless the criterion itself can be proved by a still higher criterion, the resulting "proof" is only a relative truth; true, perhaps, but not fully workable until it is confirmed by a greater light. Therefore, all a person has to do is suspend his Higher Vision if he wants to see what he wants to see and read his own meaning into every fact of life. The inclination of our souls determines whether we are self-righteous beings, "free" from Truth, fascinated and justified by scientific facts, even when we don't understand them, or free from error, thanks to the Ultimate Truth Who frees us from evil and death.

The ape-man's rejection of Reality blocks out the Ultimate Criterion by which facts can be verified. Thus, his soul remains lie-dead, inherently hungry, and desperate to hear how his ape-minded self might find a glory that he can never realize.

248

We have only two ways in which to deal with fault and guilt. One of them is to face the music and accept the guilt, and the other is to see fault as virtue and deny the guilt. The atheist-ape type, whose pridefulness obliges him to deny the evidence of failing, has a craven need to believe in a lying deliverer to save him from the shame of realizing that he will never be the god he thinks he is becoming. He glorifies those who glorify his failing, and he is justified by them in return.

Microbes, diseases, and pests evolve and thrive, despite men's efforts to thwart them, while man grows weaker in spite of his cures and potions. Drugs designed to aid people by killing germs end up favoring the pests by invoking their defense mechanisms and challenging them to fight back. Environmental stresses seem to bring out the best in the beast. Beasts adapt and grow strong, but man responds with a know-it-all, above-it-all attitude that leads to decadence.

Of course, if you have done any gardening, you know that plants do better when you care for them, rather than leave them to slug it out with weeds and other competitors. So do flocks and herds. Domestication provides protection against the various adverse evolutionary processes going on in nature's own jungle, and it produces better, more useful strains for man than he could hope to get by letting nature take its course. After all, not everything in nature acknowledges, and is grateful for, its slave relationship to man, the master.

Look carefully at nature in the raw, and you will observe a process of natural selection contributing to the process of evolution. For instance, white rabbits, being less visible to their predators than dark ones, survive a lot better than the darker rabbits in snowy Arctic regions. White may not be the ideal color in any absolute sense, but it is certainly the color that is going to survive and predominate in the polar regions.

All living beings fare better in an intelligently cultivated environment than they do in a wild jungle environment. If I lie, all farmers should walk away from their plows, throw away their hoes, and tear down their fences. But I don't lie. I see that our mistake, in an evolutionary sense, is to struggle against the symptoms of nature within us. We must return to the paradisiacal state of mind.

In the light of what I have been saying, take a good look at your own relationships, with your spouse and with others, and ask yourself whether those relationships are evolving toward perfection. How do you feel about life in general? Is it meaningful, or is it hopeless? If you see the meaninglessness of life, you are seeing two truths: one, the hopeless way of vanity, by the Light of the other, the orderly, paradisiacal way.

Unlike non-human nature, which finds all the comfort it needs in Mother Nature, "naturized" man, one who has adapted to earthy ways, finds himself in a state of conflict. He sees how the simple coming-together of male and female produces harmony in the naturally natural world, whereas it presents an ages-old mystical problem to him.

Marriage is the classic proving ground, the best place to discover the truth of our origin. Marriage becomes a heaven or a hell, depending on what we choose to believe about life. Your attitude has everything to do with the kind of woman, or man, you attract—also, with the philosophy or religion you accept. You will accept either the one that accepts you the way you are, or the one that calls you back to the way you should *be*.

If you are a proud person, you will seek support for whatever you are; you will grow to become more of that kind of person, and one day you will see that your condoning playmate is coming from hell. Do you see now why you have been unable to find your perfect soulmate? Could it be because your idea of a perfect lover has been one who would agree with everything you are, one who will keep reinforcing your ego-animal self all the way to kingdom come, or, more likely, the other place?

Whenever you say that something is evil, or bad, you are implying that you have a standard for evaluating good. The good standard outlines things as they are, so, naturally, the bad stands out. Likewise, if you say that life looks hopeless, you imply a knowledge of hope. It is only the vain path you are on, as the result of a false system of beliefs, that is hopeless. You are as deluded as the rose-colored-glasses type of positive thinker, who insists on lying to himself about life's being beautiful and perfect, with death the entrance to Heaven.

I would ask the smug evolutionist, "Are you upset that things have not turned out well for you? What heresy! How dare you entertain such a notion?" And to those who extol the evolutionary code of jungle morality, I would ask, "How can you get angry at someone for wronging you, when, by your own code, you claim that there is no right, no wrong, no absolute? How can you dare to judge?"

People seldom see the contradictions inherent in their philosophy of life. If we are nothing but a bunch of evolving creatures, we have no right to get upset with our fellow ape for acting like an ape. Under such a system, none of us can possibly be wrong, or do wrong, for we are evolving toward perfection and animal glory.

You could tell me that I am deceived. OK, let's take a look at the possibility. To be deceived, I should have had to be led astray. But who or what would want to do such a thing to me? What purpose would be served by such a deception? And why would I be stupid enough to believe a lie as a truth? If you evolutionists are right, all is as it should be, so, by your own standards, there is no such thing as deception. Of course, you might counter by calling me stubborn, now that you have lost the argument about my having been deceived. But by calling me stubborn, would you not mean that I am refusing to face reality? Again, you would have to deny your own principles to gainsay me, for, by your own code, the reality of what I have evolved to be *is the only reality* you acknowledge.

So you see, dear readers, that I have the evolutionists "hoist" by their own petard. If I am guilty of anything, it is Pride, and Pride is the very guiding light of those who disagree with my principles. If we accept the theory of evolution, we have no choice but to be what we are, so we have every right to be proud of it, to proclaim it on banners and march in defense of it, as though we were participants in a holy crusade, no matter how disgusting our cause might appear to those who see Pride as the evil it is.

You see, it is the nature of Pride to "duck" Reality,

to fail to face up to the immutable facts, to challenge every evidence of God's intention with some clever invention of failing man. The proud man even prefers the fact of death to Reality, because death *is* the reality of pride.

If we believe in the evolution of man, we can have no choice but to be what we have evolved to be. So, on what basis can we complain of our own miserable lot, or blame it on any of the rest of us? To believe in evolution is to disqualify ourselves from judging the behavior of others; yet it is obvious that we do judge and we do resent. And we can hardly find any logical basis for denying the fact that we judge because we have *reason* to judge. In other words, evil *does* exist, and deep down in your heart, regardless of your surface loyalties, you know very well that evil exists. You not only see faults in others; you often feed the error in others in order to enjoy the feeling of godhood you enjoy by judging. Why else would you weaken and spoil your own little child, and destroy his innocence? You have inherited the nature of Satan, who, through lying rhetoric, delights in seeing men stumble and fail, and laughs as he pulls the rug out from under them, the very rug that he had offered them as a flying carpet to Paradise.

Of course, the movers and shakers of the world are angry with me, because what I am saying to you threatens their entire insane system of belief. Their defensiveness proves that, despite their insistence on a relative, not-to-be judged, morality, they do have a belief system, and it is threatened by mine.

How can anyone in his right mind conclude that

there is no Truth? In view of all the careful scientific analysis and probing we engage in, how can we not see the contradiction that is inherent in such a statement? Just think: an entire lifetime of intelligent research must end in nothingness, for we cannot accept its results without contradicting our belief in their non-existence! Of course, there is a contradiction, and it is the Greater Truth, the Truth our brainy ones refuse to accept, that does the contradicting, and it is my kind of Truth. It is the Truth that prompts me to reach out to you with these lines, in the hope that they will wake you to the realization of God and sever your allegiance to the lie that has seduced you.

Man exists to know and acknowledge and live by the Truth. His reward is eternal life. His punishment for failing to do so is death.

The yearning we all feel bears witness, in itself, to the existence of a Truth we have managed to lose sight of. We are all deeply troubled, simply because we have lost contact with Reality. To the evolutionist, of course, we can not have lost sight of anything at all, inasmuch as we are still connected to our source of origin, in harmony with ourselves. But no matter how loudly the evolutionist protests, I know that Truth exists, and it is made manifest to me by the God I worship.

Governments of the world will pay millions for the bones of an original ape-man, because next to the "truth" of death is the "truth" of evolution; and just as long as such "truth" is preached and accepted, the lie that it is will make monkeys out of us all. And Hell, through governments, will continue to lord it over man in his Hell on earth.

254

In the beginning, it was an appeal to Pride that led to the existence of death. As long as man chooses to remain proud, he will be blind to Reality, and his blindness will disable him from seeing anything but a death-and-taxes kind of world. But if you will allow Reality to show you the folly of pride, and gradually strip it from your consciousness, the veil of death will lift before your eyes, and you will step into the world of infinity.

Mortal man is lie-created, lie-hungry, lie-led, and lie-dependent. The lie is the truth to him. It has to be; otherwise, his ego would be forced to see what has happened to him.

Satan, Prince of Darkness, operating through the ambitious elite, glorifies in your dying to him. He leads you, through his apostles of ambition, to himself. And he kills you through enticing you into a debilitating lifestyle, filled with lies and pleasures. As long as you believe in the lie, especially the basic one concerning evolution and death, which is simply an extension of pride, you can not find your way to Reality, to everlasting Life.

Your life depends on your seeing the truth in what I am revealing here. How can anyone believe in the evolution of man, and yet hope for salvation? From what? For if evolution were the way, there would be no need for salvation, no need for God and His saving grace.

I hope that I have disabused you of any belief you may have had in evolution, so that now, through doubting evil and believing good, you may begin your journey to the Light.

Most of us are the sum total of our experiences, but another way of saying this is that we are burdened down and bothered by our past. Unless we learn to respond properly in the present moment, the present becomes merely an extension of that burdensome past.

Roy Masters, author of this persuasive self-help book, describes a remarkably simple technique to help us face life properly, calmly. He shows us that it is the way we respond emotionally to pressures that makes us sick and depressed.

By leading us back to our center of dignity and understanding and showing us how to apply one simple principle, Roy Masters shows us how to remain sane, poised and tranquil under the most severe trials and tribulations.

Roy Masters has nothing less to offer you than the secret of life itself—how to get close to yourself and find your lost identity, the true self you have lost in the confusion.

The observation exercise materials consist of the book, *How Your Mind Can Keep You Well,* and three (3) cassettes of the same title. We suggest a donation of $30, or whatever you can afford.